THE CREDIT CARD CATASTROPHE

THE CREDIT CARD

The 20th Century Phenomenon

That Changed the World

CATASTROPHE

MATTY SIMMONS

BARRICADE BOOKS

New York

Published by Barricade Books Inc.
150 Fifth Avenue
New York, NY 10011

Book design by Cindy LaBreacht.
Printed in the United States of America.

Library of Congress Cataloging-in-Publication Data
Simmons, Matty.
    The credit card catastrophe / Matty Simmons.
    p. cm.
    ISBN 1-56980-038-3: $22.00
    1. Credit cards—United States—History. I. Title.
HG3756.U54S56 1995
332.7'65'0973—dc20   94-44571
                                              CIP

First printing

To Kate who will grow up in a world
we now can only dream about

BOOKS BY MATTY SIMMONS

ON THE HOUSE
(with Don Simmons)/Coward-McCann

THE DINERS CLUB DRINK BOOK
Doubleday/New American Library

THE BEST
(collection of short stories)/Doubleday

THE CARD CASTLE
(novel)/Putnam

IF YOU DON'T BUY THIS BOOK WE'LL
KILL THIS DOG Life, Laughs, Love and Death
at National Lampoon/Barricade Books

Table of Contents

PROLOGUE The Credit Card / **11**

CHAPTER ONE Along Came MacNamara / **15**

CHAPTER TWO What Are *We* Doing Here? / **25**

CHAPTER THREE Al Arrives, Frank Leaves / **33**

CHAPTER FOUR The Great Years / **39**

CHAPTER FIVE American Express,
The "First" Competitor / **57**

CHAPTER SIX What Are *They* Doing There? / **61**

CHAPTER SEVEN They're Off / **67**

CHAPTER EIGHT The Publicity Stunt / **85**

CHAPTER NINE The Sixties...The Best...
The Worst / **93**

CHAPTER TEN The Fat Lady Sings / **101**

CHAPTER ELEVEN The Bank Cards Arrive / **115**

CHAPTER TWELVE Clippings / **133**

CHAPTER THIRTEEN You Can See
the Twenty-First Century From Here,
and It's a Credit-Card World / **149**

CHAPTER FOURTEEN My Card Is Better
Than Your Card / **161**

CHAPTER FIFTEEN The Credit Cards
For People Who Can't Get Credit Cards / **181**

CHAPTER SIXTEEN Amex, Diners, and the
Disappearing Credit-Card Company / **187**

CHAPTER SEVENTEEN How Many Is Too Many? / **205**

CHAPTER EIGHTEEN On Spending Too Much / **213**

CHAPTER NINETEEN The Debtors / **223**

CHAPTER TWENTY "Beating the System" / **239**

CHAPTER TWENTY-ONE Will Cash Die, and Other
Opinions, Complaints, and Prognostications / **259**

CHAPTER TWENTY-TWO What I Think / **271**

CASE HISTORIES

NO. 1: Joe—The Legend / **76**

NO. 2: Phyllis—The Yogurt Queen / **97**

NO. 3: David—The Lover / **109**

NO. 4: Jimmy and Belle—The Shoppers / **128**

NO. 5: Sheri—The Girl Friend / **158**

NO. 6: Arnold—The Gambler / **178**

NO. 7: Eric—The Gourmet / **201**

NO. 8: Ben—The Shopper / **221**

NO. 9: Byron—The Swinging Banker / **237**

NO. 10: John—The Reluctant Thief / **252**

NO. 11: Roy—And the Park Avenue Apartment / **268**

Note: The stories about people and their adventures with credit cards as related in this book's case histories were either documented in print and assembled by the author or came from personal interviews. Whenever possible, real names are used. In a few cases, at the request of the individual or individuals involved, the names have been changed. Such changes are indicated by an asterisk.

THE CREDIT CARD

"A credit corresponding to his share of the annual product of the nation is given to every citizen on the public books at the beginning of each year, and a credit card issued him with which he procures at the public storehouses, found in every community, whatever he desires whenever he desires it."—Edward Bellamy, *Looking Backward: 2000 to 1887*, published 1888.

IN BELLAMY'S BOOK, a young man falls into a deep sleep and wakes up 112 years later to discover, among other things, that cash has been replaced by the credit card. Although Bellamy's foretellings haven't traveled the philosophical route he projected, certainly the credit card and the ability to "procure whatever [one] desires whenever [one] desires it" has come to be.

When Bellamy wrote his book in 1887, there were no such things as credit cards. The first large American store to introduce charge accounts was Cooperthwaite and Sons of New York City just before the turn of the century. In 1905, Spiegel began offering credit terms on everything in its catalog, and a year later, never one to let its principal competitor get too much of a jump, Sears began to sell washing machines for installments of forty-four cents a month. These were true installment plans with interest charges built in.

It is generally accepted that Western Union offered the first charge-and-settle-up-at-the-end-of-the-month plan with identification, when metal dog tags were issued to trusted customers in 1914. These were the first credit "cards." Over the next forty years or so, various types of credit identification were used including credit coins, paper scrolls, and celluloid cards.

In 1924, General Petroleum, a chain of California gas stations, issued the first cardboard credit card, calling it just that, the "General Petroleum Credit Card," using, for the first time, the name that Bellamy had given his cards thirty-six years earlier. Mobil Oil and Shell soon followed suit.

By the late 1930s, credit cards were issued by department stores, and after World War II, the airlines joined to create the Universal Air Travel Plan, a cooperative venture which included nearly every carrier in the world. Members, usually corporations, would put up a deposit of $425 and get an unlimited number of credit cards and one single monthly bill for all charges.

Of course, many individual establishments had credit cards or charge accounts in the late 1940s. If you were a bon vivant who regularly toured New York's glossier restaurants and nightclubs, for example, you might carry a credit card from the Longchamps chain or, more likely, simply have your name on file at Toots Shor's or at the Latin Quarter so you could sign your tab. Then you might get any number of bills at the end of the month. If you were not a regular or if the proprietor didn't want to set up a billing and collection system, you carried cash and if you ran out, you went home. Unless you specifically requested one, you got no receipt for a business lunch or dinner. Taxes, substantially increased to support the war, were still high, and entertainment spending for business was deductible, but bookkeeping for this purpose was haphazard as were records at most corporations for entertainment expenditures.

There was an idea in there somewhere. And Frank X. MacNamara was the guy who came up with it.

Chapter One

ALONG CAME MACNAMARA

THE AFTERNOON OF February 8, 1950, was not especially one you'd remember in New York. It was winter-cold and dark, a sullen, humorless day when you hurried into subways or onto buses or taxis anxious to go from one enclosed area to another without having too much to do with northeastern weather.

The *New York Times* sold for a nickel, and on this day it revealed, among other things, that the U.S. was now officially recognizing Vietnam, Laos, and Cambodia. The Third Avenue Transit Bus System had requested a fare increase from five to ten cents. Ted Williams, considered by many the finest batsman in baseball history, had signed his 1950 contract with the Boston Red Sox for a record $125,000. On the editorial pages, several letters harangued the president, Harry S Truman.

In the society columns, lengthy coverage was accorded a tea party given by former first lady Eleanor Roosevelt.

15

The advertisements let you know you could buy a new Dodge for $1,645, a bottle of Old Forester for $6.12, the *South Pacific* cast album for $4.85, and a full-course dinner at the Horn and Hardart Automat for ninety cents. A six-pack of Coca-Cola cost twenty-five cents.

You could see Judy Holliday in *Born Yesterday* on Broadway and pay $2.40 for orchestra seats. The cover charge at the Plaza Hotel's Rendezvous Room was a buck fifty.

A five-room garden duplex on Eighty-seventh Street and Park Avenue rented for $200 a month; the same amount being offered for secretarial positions in the *Times*' want-ad pages.

Bloomingdale's advertised its new "Buy now! Pay later" budget accounts, and you could also open a regular charge account which obligated you to pay within thirty days of purchase.

That day, three of us sat at a table in Major's Cabin Grill, a Manhattan restaurant on Thirty-third Street, a hundred yards or so west of Fifth Avenue, in the lengthy shadow of the Empire State Building. Major's was a businessman's restaurant, jammed at lunchtime and empty at night. I had dined there several times before with Frank MacNamara and Ralph Schneider but this day—this lunch—this moment—was to be something special. The waiter handed MacNamara the tab. He looked at it, then returned it with one hand and held out a small card with the other.

The waiter studied the card carefully. At first he wasn't quite sure what to make of it, then he apparently remembered a speech the restaurant's owner, Major

Satz, had given to his serving staff that morning. He nodded and left, bill and card in hand. The three of us at the table smiled apprehensively. Was this actually going to happen? The waiter returned with a three-part slip that had been given him by the cashier. MacNamara signed it, added a sizable tip, kept one of the parts, and turned to us and grinned.

"Goddamn it!" he said with the pride of a man who was sure he'd done something important. "It worked!"

It was the world's first credit-card charge of its kind. The stores and restaurants that had charge accounts at that time offered them only for their individual establishment or chain. This was the first time that a card had been issued by a credit-card company that would be honored at many different establishments and would result in the cardholder getting a single monthly bill that could be paid with one check.

To Frank MacNamara, who had conceived the one card/one bill plan, it was an idea that had potential, and he believed someday the card would be honored at restaurants all over New York City. *Restaurants*—thus the name Diners Club. To Ralph Schneider, his lawyer and friend, it had been one of the rare MacNamara ideas that made any sense. Schneider had invested ten thousand dollars in the scheme while MacNamara had put up only eight thousand dollars.

MacNamara had kept 90 percent of the stock in the new company since he was going to run the whole thing. Schneider was there for legal advice and to lend an ear. He had a busy law practice that occupied his time, and he had no desire to manage any business other than his own.

I had met the two men only a few months earlier.

In 1950, I was a twenty-three-year-old press agent. My brother, Don, nearly five years older than me, was my partner. Our clients included the Ford Television Hour, one of the first big network variety shows; the bandleader Artie Shaw; folk singer Josh White; and such varied accounts as the Henry Hudson Hotel and a newly imported beer from Holland, Heineken.

Most of our accounts, however, were restaurants and nightclubs ranging from the chic Club Bagatelle and Embassy Club to Phil Gluckstern's Kosher Restaurant and the expensive Café Chambord, considered at the time to be the most elegant dining place in New York. We were doing well. It seemed we worked all the time, everyday, nearly every hour.

We had only crossed over the Brooklyn Bridge to arrive at where we were in 1950, but for a couple of Depression-reared kids who had shared a living-room couch in a three-bedroom apartment for which our father, the proprietor of the Flatbush Sign Company, paid a hard-to-come-by thirty-five-dollars-a-month rental, we had traveled to the opposite end of the earth.

I had been a copyboy for the *New York World-Telegram*, then briefly a reporter at age eighteen before being drafted into the army during World War II, where for almost two years I was in charge of entertainment at Fort Monmouth in New Jersey. My brother, who joined the merchant marine at the outset of the war, had been torpedoed three times. At Monmouth I invited an up-and-coming young singer named Vic Damone to come out and entertain the troops. He arrived with his manager and his press agent, a fellow Brooklynite named

Sid Ascher, who invited me to look him up when I got out of the army.

When I did, in 1946, I called Ascher and he offered me a job writing jokes for Walter Winchell, Earl Wilson, and other columnists. These would be credited to his clients and would appear in print as their bright, witty remarks. My salary—thirty dollars a week.

After three months of this, I ran into another press agent named Ernie Brooks. He was the resident publicist for a supper club called El Borracho. Ernie said he knew a woman who was opening a restaurant to be called Lilliana's in Greenwich Village. He could get me the account, he suggested. It would pay forty bucks a week. He would get a commission of ten dollars payable in cash each week in front of the hotel in which he lived— the Belmont Plaza on Lexington Avenue and Forty-ninth Street. In addition to the forty, I would be given free dinner every evening, but I would be expected to remain on the premises until the dinner crowd left.

I quit my job, taking with me what I learned—primarily how to communicate with the all-powerful New York columnists. A month or so later, my brother Don left the merchant marine and joined me. Sitting alone at his typewriter, he mastered the knack of writing in the style of each columnist. While I was out meeting people and making both notes and friends, he'd do what I did at Ascher's office. He'd write gags and create fictitious news items which would then appear in the columns. People started to pay attention to us.

Ernie Brooks moved up both geographically (Fifty-fifth Street to Sixtieth Street) and in esteem, leaving El Borracho and now publicizing the swank and very exclusive Colony Restaurant. I replaced him at El Borracho. The fee, which I split with my brother, was fifty dollars a week. I still got a free dinner and was still expected to be on hand each evening, and Ernie would still get his ten-dollars-a-week commission, but it was different here. Celebrities abounded and the columnists came by on their nightly rounds. Now, my brother and I were both writing all day, and El Borracho was getting the kind of wide press coverage usually reserved for the Stork Club or El Morocco or Toots Shor's, New York's most famous watering holes. We'd often write full columns for Winchell or society columnist Cholly Knickerbocker (Igor Cassini) and others.

Over the next year, other accounts wanted us to work for them. I told Nicky Quattrociocchi, the proprietor of El Borracho, that we could no longer be his press agents exclusively.

By January of 1950, Don and I were operating one of the most successful publicity outfits in the city. A good friend, Eddie Black, wrote a restaurant column and sold advertising for the Hearst New York afternoon newspaper, the Journal-American. Eddie often recommended us to potential clients, and now he called to ask if I would meet a man he knew who had an unusual idea. The man wanted to issue a credit card that would be honored at New York restaurants.

This fellow had two problems: he didn't know how to sell the plan to the public, and he had limited contacts in the restaurant industry. That meant that he would be soliciting restaurants that didn't have the slightest idea who he was. He'd try to persuade them to issue credit to customers that would be paid by him at a later date. He'd tried with a number of restaurants, and he'd struck out everywhere.

I wasn't enthusiastic, but as a favor to Eddie, I agreed to meet with Frank MacNamara at his Empire State Building office.

Many years later I would become a film producer. If I were casting the part of a traditional used-car salesman, someone who looked like he would sell you a car without a motor, it would be Frank MacNamara.

Frank, at thirty-three, was pudgy with slick black hair and a pencil-thin mustache. He was very friendly. He greeted me warmly then got up from his desk and called into an adjacent office. Soon a small, dapper man, deeply tanned and with a nose that had obviously been broken somewhere along the way, came in and shook my hand. This was Ralph E. Schneider. Six years older than MacNamara and with a Harvard law degree hanging on the wall of his office, he let MacNamara do most of the talking.

First, MacNamara held up a small piece of cardboard. Across one side, in roughly drawn script were the words, "Diners Club." He then explained what his idea was. One card. Many restaurants. One monthly bill.

"It's perfect for the businessman," he enthused. "You pay all your business entertainment with one monthly check. You don't have to carry a lot of cash with you, and, most importantly, you have receipts for reimbursement from your firm and entertainment receipts for tax deductions."

I listened unimpressed. He went on. "It's all of those things," he said, "but maybe most importantly, it's prestige. It's having a good enough credit rating to own one of these cards so that restaurants will treat you like somebody who's somebody. If you're a businessman and you're entertaining clients or working on a deal, the people with you will be impressed."

MacNamara really was in love with his idea. He went on with great enthusiasm. "We're only going to give these cards to people of substance. Let's face it! They're going to owe us money. We'll have to pay the restaurants even if we don't get paid by the cardholder."

"How do you make your money?" I asked.

"We collect 100 percent from the cardholder and reimburse the restaurant at 94 percent."

I digested this. "You're going to keep six percent of the tab?"

Again he nodded.

I pondered. "That could be a tough sell," I said.

Schneider, as slow and deliberate as MacNamara was quick, for the first time added to the mix. "Frank believes that someone charging for food and drink will spend more money than if he had to pay with cash, with 'real money.'"

"And," I asked, "do you charge the cardholder anything?"

"No," MacNamara answered firmly. "Nobody would pay to get a credit card."

I left that day without a great deal of interest in their desire to have me promote their idea. I had never charged anything in my life. In addition, I was leery. This new enterprise was hardly substantial. The company that would father the Diners Club was the Hamilton Credit Corporation of which MacNamara was the sole owner until Schneider invested his ten thousand dollars. Hamilton's business was loaning money to small companies. Before that, MacNamara had owned a canvas-manufacturing company. Schneider had entered private law practice after years with the Office of Price Administration (price controls) during World War II. They were hardly kings of industry. (I didn't then know that their total original investment was only eighteen thousand dollars. If I had, I would have been even more dubious.)

What concerned me most was that I would be asked not only to publicize this new conception but to persuade restaurants to honor it. Don and I now represented ten of Manhattan's important dining and drinking places. By asking them to participate, we'd be putting ourselves on the line. For example, what if this glib Irishman collected cardholder money and disappeared?

Another thing that bothered me was that there were no marketing people involved. This was an idea that had to be sold, and publicity was only one way. Someone had to create advertising, perhaps direct mail, and conceive other ways, new ways to reach the cardholder.

MacNamara, of course, knew that, too. He'd neglected to tell me that I was the person he had in mind not only to publicize the new plan but to market it.

Chapter Two
WHAT ARE WE DOING HERE?

FRANK CALLED ME frequently over the next couple of weeks, and I kept putting him off, telling him I wasn't sure I was the right man for the job. He was as persistent as he was persuasive, and he kept calling and telling me about the wonderful potential of the credit card. "Someday," he predicted, "restaurants all over New York will honor this card."

I doubted it. I kept putting him off. Then, one day, my brother looked up from his typewriter and asked, "Have you ever heard of Edward Bellamy?"

I thought for a moment. "The nineteenth-century visionary? The guy who peered into the twentieth century and predicted things to come?"

Don nodded. Sequestered on merchant ships for months at a time during the war, he'd read hundreds of books. He was referring to one called *Looking Backward*. In it Bellamy predicted a monetary system based on the credit card. No cash. Everybody had a credit card, and you could pay for anything you wanted with it.

I looked at him and shook my head. "This one won't be easy," I said.

He shrugged.

Two days later I reached an agreement with MacNamara. Our fee would be $200 a week plus a promise that if this worked, I would get a small piece of the new company.

When I asked MacNamara how he thought of the idea, he smiled and said, "I just get ideas. I write them down and think about them for a while. Then I throw out the ones that don't float. This one was never discarded."

That wouldn't do. I had to glamorize the creation of the credit-card plan, so I came up with a story of how he'd been entertaining a business acquaintance in a restaurant and asked for the tab. When it came, he discovered that he hadn't brought enough cash. Rather than embarrass himself in front of the man he'd invited to dinner, he called his wife who drove in from their Long Island home, cash in hand. While he waited, he decided that this sort of thing should never happen, that a responsible businessman should be able to sign a restaurant tab everywhere.

My story has appeared literally thousands of times in newspapers and magazines and books all over the world. In a beautiful four-color brochure, the Diners Club still evokes the legend of MacNamara sitting in that restaurant—his dining partner long gone—waiting for his wife and dreaming of a credit-card world.

Of course, they couldn't know until reading this that the scene never took place.

MacNamara and Schneider ate lunch daily at Major's Cabin Grill, and because of this, Major's was the first restaurant to agree to honor Diners Club cards. Part of my assignment was to add to that lonely list. The Chambord, Bagatelle, Embassy Club, Gluckstern's, and Jimmy Kelly's—all clients of mine—agreed to participate, albeit begrudgingly. With these names in hand, MacNamara went out and persuaded Townley's, the Prince George Hotel dining rooms, and several others that they too should join the experiment.

A card was designed and printed and sent, unsolicited, to several thousand prominent businessmen with a letter revealing its wonders. There was no fee for membership.

When Frank MacNamara signed his name on that tab at Major's Cabin Grill that February day, I felt, for the first time, an enthusiasm that I hadn't felt before. What if MacNamara's little scheme worked and spread to restaurants, not just all over New York but all over the country? Hell, what if Edward Bellamy's prognostications came to be, and someday you'd be able to charge damn near everything, damn near everywhere? Nah, I told myself. It would never happen. Cash is king and always will be.

The publicity began. Stories appeared in every major New York newspaper, and our small office in the Empire State Building was flooded with letters and calls requesting the free card. Applications were checked out, and cards were issued only to people with substantial incomes and verified bank accounts.

Within months, the Diners Club moved to a larger office in the Empire State Building. Over the next two years, it would move three more times to bigger quarters in the same building.

MacNamara made several other moves. The six percent being charged to restaurants would not do it, he decided. After the first two dozen or so establishments signed, the fee to all new signees was raised to seven percent.

He also hired a man named Dick Kirkpatrick who, in a matter of weeks, created a simple bookkeeping process for sorting and billing charges and paying the restaurants. Since the computer was still in its infancy, everything was done by hand. In later years, we were to discover that Kirkpatrick's manual systems were more accurate and certainly more profitable than the early computers installed in the sixties.

Requests for cardholder memberships continued to pour in. Now, the national press was poking around and stories in *Business Week*, *Time*, and *Newsweek* swelled membership. By the fall of 1950, restaurants in New York, Chicago, Boston, Philadelphia, Miami, and Los Angeles were honoring the card. Cardholders numbered nearly thirty thousand, and they were using the cards to charge $250,000 a month. The company was grossing, from its percentage, more than $16,000 a month.

And it was losing money.

Factors—moneylenders who loan money for commercial ventures—were now involved because money had to be paid to the establishments before it was collected from the cardholders. Their interest rates and the increasing cost of operations were not being met by the percentage of charges.

The three of us caucused. "Why not," I suggested, "charge for the card?" MacNamara shook his head. "Nobody," he again said, "will pay for a credit card."

But Schneider wasn't sure. "I don't know," he said. "I have a hunch we'd lose the people who don't use the card, but the people who do won't mind paying a small fee."

I wrote a letter to the cardholders, explaining our problem. We had to charge to be able to continue to give them this service. We were instituting a three-dollar membership fee.

When we analyzed the reaction to the new fee, we found that, as Schneider had predicted, only nonusers of the card dropped out. The people who used the card paid for it at once.

The Diners Club was not to have another losing year for the next seventeen years. The fee and the weeding out of nonusing members made it a sure winner.

The publicity was really paying off. By year-end 1950, the original staff of three plus MacNamara had expanded to twenty-three. The moves to larger space couldn't be made quickly enough to house the expanding number of people hired to check credit, sort bills, answer inquiries, and pay the establishments.

Schneider had by now just about abandoned his law practice. He urged caution. "Take more time. Slow down on new memberships until we can adjust to this kind of growth." But MacNamara would have none of it, and he kept pushing. Clerks worked sixteen-hour shifts, and he'd be right in the middle of them, shuffling paper and answering the constantly ringing phones. Meanwhile, he urged me to create newspaper and magazine ads and, finally, direct mail. By the spring of 1951, membership exceeded 100,000. Nearly that many had applied for a Diners Club card and been rejected because they were poor credit risks. Credit losses were running at 1/4 of 1 percent. At that point the largest tab any member had signed for was $496.

The Henry Hudson Hotel extended the right to charge rooms to members so it was literally no longer merely, a "Diners" club, but, then again, it wasn't really a club either. Other hotels quickly followed suit. Budget Rent-a-Car agreed to become the first car-rental system to honor the card.

Member establishments now participated in every major city in the United States, and cardholder membership was coming in from outside the U.S.

The "Diners Club News," a newsletter I created, was stuffed into the bills going to members. It became so popular (and profitable because of restaurant advertising) that it was upgraded and enlarged. It became the *Diners Club Magazine*. To get second-class postage rates, we needed to charge for it, so we added one dollar to the annual membership fee, raising it to four dollars. Members were told to check a box if they didn't want the magazine. Few people get around to saying they don't want something, and more than 90 percent of the membership subscribed to the magazine which grew as quickly as the credit card itself and, for a while, proved nearly as profitable.

As anticipated, competitors surfaced. An outfit called Trip-Charge popped up out of Chicago, and a group headquartered in New York and Los Angeles introduced Dine and Sign whose principals included the department-store heir, Broadway and film producer, and playboy, Alfred Bloomingdale.

But the Diners Club was growing so quickly and to such acclaim that competition was dismissed airily. MacNamara's verve did not cloak an arrogance that suggested that he was on a roll—everybody step aside.

The first card that had been issued by the Diners Club was number 1000 which MacNamara took for himself. Schneider had number 1001, and I had number 1002. In 1951 that was the pecking order. It would soon change.

Chapter Three

AL ARRIVES, FRANK LEAVES

ONE COULD NOT imagine two more less likely partners than Frank MacNamara and Ralph E. Schneider. Where Frank was mercurial, Ralph was downright laconic. He had heavy eyelids and always looked as though he was falling asleep. Both were married and each had two children. Surprisingly, the unorthodox MacNamara was much more of a family man than Schneider whose bedroom eyes invariably fixed on any attractive woman in a room. Women found him fascinating, and soon after the Diners Club began, he entered into a series of dalliances that eventually destroyed his marriage.

At work, Schneider was the stable member of the two, and a strange turnaround in ownership of the Diners Club started to take place. MacNamara had agreed at the outset of the company to draw a small salary. Suddenly, he was the much-publicized president of this new phenomena and was bound to the same income. Money couldn't be taken out in dividends without his partner's approval, and that wasn't forthcoming because the company needed to use its profits for its ever-expanding cash demands. The faster the credit-card business grew, the more money had to be paid to establishments before collecting from cardholders.

But MacNamara wanted to live like the runaway success the press was describing. Early on, Schneider came up with a plan. MacNamara would draw cash from the business, and Schneider would draw a like amount in stock. In addition, Schneider would start working actively on Diners Club business. By 1952, the ninety/ten split in ownership had become a fifty/fifty partnership. MacNamara's promise that I would become a participant wasn't fulfilled until the company went public.

MacNamara was not a fool, merely someone who guessed wrong. By 1952, membership was up to 150,000. He'd put his own personal ceiling on the company's growth and thought that it would be reached soon.

Dine and Sign and Trip-Charge were both floundering. Schneider met with Bloomingdale and his partners and agreed to acquire their company for a small interest in the Diners Club. Bloomingdale also invested twenty-five thousand dollars for another fractional interest. He was immediately made vice-president in charge of western operations, and a second billing and credit office was opened in Los Angeles under his supervision.

In mid-1952, Bloomingdale and Schneider bought out MacNamara's 50 percent interest in the company for $500,000. Bloomingdale became president of the company while Schneider, who had no title while MacNamara was president, became chairman and, more importantly, chief operating officer. It was clearly understood that he was "the boss."

"It won't last," MacNamara, the man who invented the credit card and who had seemed to once have boundless enthusiasm for his idea, now told me as he packed the personal belongings in his office into crates. "It'll peter out at 250,000 members, last for a while, then disappear like the zoot suit."

Then he told me something I'd never forget. "You know," he said, "if Ralph hadn't objected, I would have fired you a long time ago. You've done a great job, but publicity and marketing people should be changed regularly to get new ideas and enthusiasm into the company."

A year later, membership passed the 300,000 mark. My enthusiasm wouldn't ebb for fifteen years. The company would go public and, eventually, MacNamara's original 90 percent ownership would be roughly valued at fifty million dollars, one hundred times the figure he'd sold out for. Nineteen fifty-three was the year I left the publicity business and came to the Diners Club exclusively. I would be executive vice-president in charge of sales and marketing and also editor-in-chief of the *Diners Club Magazine*. My brother Don now became the sole proprietor of our public relations firm.

Ralph Schneider was the perfect man for the job of controlling this runaway business. He originated virtually nothing. He just saw to it that nobody screwed things up.

Credit losses were up somewhat to 1/2 of 1 percent, but the membership fee was now six dollars, including that dollar for the magazine, and profits were rising as rapidly as memberships. Schneider and I had become close friends even though I had married and he had been divorced and was now a swinging bachelor. I was the only one to whom he gave an almost totally free rein in the company.

I opened branch offices all over the U.S. and Canada. We had popularized the "take-one box" you find on restaurant and hotel counters, and I hired an energetic sales manager named Bill Richman who had an army of salesmen installing the boxes of brochures and applications in both countries. It now passed direct mail as our principal source of new membership. The magazine had become an invaluable tool for signing new establishments and as a buffer for tirades against the 7 percent cut we took on charges. We'd sign a hotel chain, and as part of the deal, give them two or more pages of free advertising in our magazine, which had become the most responsive travel and dining publication in America. I wrote a restaurant column in the magazine under the pen name Franco Borghese. A review in the column would jam a restaurant for weeks and calm any complaint about our percentage of the charges.

We loaned money to restaurants. Since we'd started, the Stork Club had refused to honor the Diners Club card. Finally, Bloomingdale, one of the café circuit's favorite customers, arranged for me to meet with the club's legendary proprietor, Sherman Billingsley. Billingsley was still reluctant, feeling it would diminish the exclusivity his restaurant was so famous for. I offered him advertising. He wasn't persuaded. "What do you need?" I asked finally.

"I need money," he said.

I advanced him fifty thousand dollars against future Diners Club charges, and he signed a contract.

Shortly after, I made the same deal with Toots Shor's.

By the end of the decade, membership was past the one-million mark. The company, now listed on the New York Stock Exchange, was showing profits of five million dollars a year. Early competitors like Trip-Charge, the Duncan Hines Signet Club, and the Esquire Club had either faded away or, like Dine and Sign, been acquired. A more formidable competitor, American Express, had entered the credit-card field in 1958, but the Diners Club was still the strong number one.

Our card was now honored all over the world. After signing France as the first international franchise in 1955, an enterprising Diners Club vice-president named M. Mark Sulkes sold franchises for every country except the United States and Canada which, of course, were owned by the original Diners Club.

You could use your card to charge flowers through the giant FTD system or at gas stations, liquor stores, for part-time help and chauffeured limos as well as for car rentals.

As the competition for cardholders with American Express heated up and the wonders of credit-card life were exposed to more people, membership grew at its fastest pace since the very first years.

Frank MacNamara had a new ambition when he collected his $500,000 check. He would get into real estate and building. Housing, he told us, was where to put your money. Build for the Baby Boomers. He built a development in Pennsylvania. When construction was completed, it was discovered that the homes had limited access to household water. It made the houses uninhabitable. He lost the $500,000 he collected on the sale of his Diners Club stock. He'd been right about housing in the fifties and sixties. Families were expanding, and people were buying homes in suburban and rural communities.

Once again Frank had a good idea—but something had gone wrong.

On November 9, 1957, he suffered a heart attack and died at the age of forty. He was broke.

In a 1990 review of "The Most Important Americans of the Twentieth Century," *Life* magazine ran a picture of Frank MacNamara dining at a restaurant. It was accompanied by the fiction I'd created of Frank being stranded without his money and coming up with "the cashless society."

Chapter Four

THE GREAT YEARS

TO BE INVOLVED with a booming success like the Diners Club gives one a feeling hard to describe. Using sports as an analogy, it's like being in the Super Bowl or winning the batting title, except, in the case of the Diners Club, the euphoria lasted not days or weeks but years. For more than ten years, it seemed that we could do no wrong. Even when we made mistakes, they worked. When we guessed, we guessed right. When, in the late fifties, American Express and Hilton's Carte Blanche, our first major competitors, moved onto the credit-card scene, we were still omniscient. We outsmarted them, outhustled them, and outlucked them.

We were on a roll, and it was great fun. When you got up in the morning, you looked forward to going to the office to see what good fortune would come your way that day.

Our farflung network of sales offices were reeling in members in astonishing numbers. Joe Titus, who in the

early fifties was named vice-president of credit operations, had a tight control on the issuance of the cards
and on collections. Not until American Express really
got in gear in the 1960s and in the battle for cardholders were membership requirements lowered. Only then,
did credit losses reach the 1 percent of billing mark. It
still remained a card basically for people who could
afford to carry what amounted to a blank check.

There were, of course, problems, but they were the
kind of problems that made the job interesting, perhaps
because in the fifties we were great problem solvers.

The 7 percent cut the Diners Club took before paying its cardholder's charges was a source of constant
complaint. "It's a cross we're going to have to bear," the
owner of Atlanta's popular Dale's Cellar restaurant told
Newsweek. Others were not as willing to go along.
What we feared most was restaurants forming groups
or associations to try to force us to lower the rate. In the
late fifties, the membership fee was still $5 plus $1
(later $2). For an additional card charged to the same
account (aptly called an "add-on") for a spouse or a
member of the same firm whose bill was being paid by
one check, there was a $2.50 charge. There were no
penalty or interest charges for payments made after
thirty days. The 7 percent was still the principal source
of our income, and any request to reduce it was firmly
refused.

Crisis calls came on the same day from our sales
representatives in Seattle and Milwaukee. In both
cities, the best restaurants had organized and were
demanding a reduction in the discount rate, stating

that they would exit the Diners Club *en masse* if an immediate cut wasn't made.

If all the better restaurants in a city dropped out, their customers would simply have to pay cash. One or two restaurants leaving alone would be at a competitive disadvantage; they would not be able to offer the convenience and service of the credit card to be found at another establishment. A successful organized boycott could literally have us at the mercy of the restaurant owners and could spread throughout the world.

A survey I commissioned in the midfifties bore out what we had always maintained: a Diners Club credit cardholder spent 18 percent more than a cash customer. This, we argued, more than compensated for the 7 percent tariff.

But the restaurant groups wouldn't listen to this argument. They demanded a rate cut.

I flew to Milwaukee with one plan in mind: divide and, hopefully, conquer.

The director of the Milwaukee Restaurant Association invited me to speak at a specially called meeting. I arrived two days early and spent those two days meeting privately with owners of the leading restaurants. I offered advertising and publicity in the *Diners Club Magazine* and full-page ads in the Milwaukee papers which would list and describe the attractions of those who would stay with us. In some cases, I agreed to advance needed funds against future charges by cardholders.

On the day of the meeting, there were several fiery speeches from the proprietors who had instigated the proposed boycott, people I had carefully avoided meeting with. Finally, one got personal. "I'll be goddamned," he said, "if I'm going to pay this kind of money to make Alfred Bloomingdale even richer than he is."

The room went silent. Before I could answer, Mokey Friedman, the owner of the well-known Eugene's Restaurant in the city, slowly got to his feet.

"I've known Al Bloomingdale for years," he said. "I knew Al when he'd pay a thousand bucks just to watch two flies fuck. He doesn't need our money. I'm not dropping out."

The room erupted into laughter. When a vote was taken shortly after, all but the two proprietors who had initiated the move stayed in the Diners Club, without a cut in rates.

News of the settlement of the already widely publicized "strike" went out on the wire services and appeared in newspapers throughout the country. The problem in Seattle evaporated.

I ran the advertising and restaurant reviews I'd promised in the *Diners Club Magazine* and several full-page ads in the Milwaukee papers. It was the last uprising in the fifties.

In the midfifties, a young man by the name of Victor Lownes came to see me. He worked with Hugh Hefner who in 1953 had started a publication called *Playboy*. It had a vast circulation, but no national advertisers would even meet with him because of the magazine's nude photos and explicit stories about sex. I admired the *Playboy* approach. For the first time, sex in a magazine was being treated with class. I agreed to advertise and mentioned it to Schneider who wasn't sure.

"People will complain," he said, echoing the archaic moral standards of the time.

"The way I see it," I reasoned, "the people who buy the magazine sure as hell won't mind, and the people who don't, won't see it." It was the same "If you use it, you'll like it," philosophy Ralph had come up with for charging a membership fee. We became *Playboy*'s first national advertiser.

Jimmy Breslin was one of the country's most widely read columnists. Much of what he wrote about involved friends who were bookies, gamblers, racketeers, thugs, et al, with a murderer or two occasionally thrown into the mix for variety. I had known Breslin for years, and he was a particularly good friend of my brother's, the two of them sharing an affinity for drinks and story-telling at Jim Downey's bar and steak house on Eighth Avenue in midtown Manhattan.

"Matty," Breslin said to me one day on the phone, "I gotta see you right away! Now!"

I explained that I was busy, had several meetings that day, and asked if we couldn't make it some other time. He persisted and I invited him to my office. In the midfifties, the Diners Club had moved from the Empire State Building which had run out of contiguous space for us, and we now occupied two cavernous floors in the Coliseum office building at 10 Columbus Circle on Fifty-ninth Street.

Jimmy's large body rumbled through my office door within the hour. "I got a problem," he told me. I have always enjoyed listening to Jimmy speak, perhaps because he has preserved a New York idiom that reminds me of my youth in Brooklyn but not much of the New York of today. "It's Fat Thomas," he went on. There was a pause as though I was expected to know what Fat Thomas's problem was.

He explained. Fat Thomas was a 300-pound bookie featured in many of Jimmy's columns. It seemed that a customer had welshed on some money he owed Thomas for horses who were apparently too old to finish their races. When Thomas asked for his money, the bettor revealed that he was temporarily out of funds. The obese one then suggested that if payment was not forthcoming, he would break things—like the man's arms and legs.

The gambler could painfully picture this, so he came up with a quick solution. His markers totaled somewhere around two thousand dollars. He handed Fat Thomas his Diners Club card and suggested that he treat himself to some dinners and whatever else he should come up with that added up to the amount owed. The bookie accepted the card and in three days had wined and dined himself, assorted racetrack characters, and other shadowy individuals, running up some six thousand dollars in charges.

Meanwhile, the reluctant benefactor called the Diners Club, reported the card stolen, and took off for parts unknown.

Joe Titus's security men found Fat Thomas surrounded by friends and three or four chorus girls at a Long Island nightclub. They had already emptied a half dozen or so bottles of champagne, and Fat Thomas himself was well into his third steak. One of the security men identified himself as the club's manager and asked politely if Thomas was going to pay for this with cash or credit card. The credit card was whipped out with a flourish. "Charge it to my account, my man!" declared the bookie. He was promptly arrested and charged with possession and use of a stolen credit card. At the time of Breslin's telling of the story, he was out on bail.

I looked at Jimmy. "He owes us six grand," I said. "Does he have it?"

"No," said Breslin matter-of-factly. "He's had a bad run and he, too, is temporarily out of funds. But," said Breslin, "I have a plan. For years you and your brother have been trying to get me to write for the *Diners Club Magazine.* If you let Thomas off the hook, I'll write six stories for you at a thousand a pop, and you keep the money to pay off the credit-card bill."

This sounded like a good deal to me. Breslin's rate for magazine articles was much higher than that. I agreed. Our attorneys went to Fat Thomas's trial, explained what had transpired to the judge, and Thomas was a free man. "But," said the judge, pointing to Breslin who sat in the spectator seats, "I'll be keeping an eye on this to make sure you deliver the stories."

A few weeks later, I ran into a magazine editor I knew at Downey's. I told him the Breslin-Fat Thomas story. He laughed. "Breslin never delivers," he said. "He takes advances for stories that he doesn't write, sometimes for years."

I kept calling Jimmy. Finally, after months of pursuing him, Breslin's first story arrived in the mail. Months later, another came. A year went by and no more stories. I wrote it off as a deal that didn't work.

One day I walked into Downey's, and Breslin was sitting at the bar. He waved me over. "You know," he told me, "I ran into the judge who presided at Fat Thomas's trial." He sipped his drink and shook his head sadly. "He hated that last piece I wrote for you."

"Deep in our cultural heritage is the feeling that a man should not live beyond his means," wrote Lawrence Lackey, dean of the School of Commerce at the University of Southern California in 1954. "From Ben Franklin's *Poor Richard* to Mark Twain's *Pudd'nhead Wilson*, we have been told that the thrifty man pays his own way."

By the end of the fifth decade of the twentieth century, it had become clear that man might continue to pay his own way, but he'd pay it later.

We'd shown America you could do anything with the magic card when on a popular television show, *The Big Program*, we'd sent a winning couple completely around the world, with stopovers at hotels and restaurants and for shopping at key cities everywhere, armed only with a Diners Club card.

In 1958, *Time* magazine noted that "In the nation's expense-account economy, nobody is anybody unless he can say, 'charge it.'"

By 1960, Al Bloomingdale would predict, with a burst of sagacity, "There will be only two classes of people—those with credit cards and those who can't get them."

Of course, that was in 1960, when there were still a lot of people who couldn't get them.

By the late fifties, we had opened the outlets that honored the Diners Club card to include stores and the airlines. Here were big and profitable charges; not an eighteen-dollar or twenty-five-dollar restaurant tab but a four-or five-hundred-dollar airline ticket or a two-hundred-dollar suit. For airlines the fee was dropped to four percent because of the size of the charge. We were now about to become the universal credit card. You could charge not only while there but to get there.

The Diners Club today says that Western Airlines was the first to honor the card. They may be right since I was unable to find documentation on a date, but I recall it differently, mostly because I remember the day I made the first deal with an airline and what happened during those negotiations.

An affable, enterprising man named Jim Austin was the president of Northeast Airlines in 1958. The airline did much of its business in the northeastern United States but had recently been awarded both the Boston and New York routes to Miami. In the 1950s, Florida was, by far, America's major vacation mecca, and the air traffic between the northeast and Miami was prodigious. Eastern Airlines had long had a lock on the routes. Now, Northeast, a small operator in the airline industry, suddenly became a player. After several meetings, Jim Austin was interested in making a deal.

The two of us sat alone in the boardroom at the Diners Club, working on an agreement. We'd been at it no more than a few minutes when Schneider opened the door and stuck his head into the room. I hurriedly introduced him to Jim and, expecting him to leave, resumed our discussion.

He didn't leave.

"Matty," he said softly. "Can I see you for a moment?"

I was astonished. I was working on a deal that could

send us feet first into the airline industry. It was, perhaps, the most important negotiation in the history of the Diners Club to date. But this was the chairman.

I spoke as softly as he had. "Ralph, could we talk later? Jim and I are into this."

He fidgeted. "Well," he said, "I really want to talk to you now. It'll only take a minute."

Suddenly, it struck me that perhaps someone had died or the government had declared war on credit cards or some equal devastation. I excused myself and followed him out of the room. Alone in the hallway, he held out an envelope and showed it to me. "There's a first-class stamp on this envelope," he said. "It could have been sent third class."

My mouth dropped. I looked at him like he was crazy. This was the Harvard lawyer whose common sense and firm but low-key management had taken Frank MacNamara's idea to legendary heights. What was being negotiated in the boardroom meant millions in charges and profits, new boundaries for the credit card. What he held in his hand involved a nickel. If a hundred such letters were involved, it meant five dollars.

I couldn't speak. A guttural roar literally burst from my mouth. He shrugged. "It's the principal of the thing," he said.

I went back and closed the deal. Ralph and I never discussed the price of stamps again.

The next day, I called the president of Eastern Airlines. "I just signed Northeast Airlines to a Diners Club contract," I told him. "Do you want all of our one million businessmen and travelers to use only Northeast on your common routes?"

A week later, I signed Eastern. The rest of the airline industry fell into place soon after.

When we started in 1950, the list of restaurants honoring the Diners Club card easily fit on the back of the cardboard credit card. When those numbers grew, we printed the card on an accordion pullout, and there were seven pages of listings. The next step was a booklet with the credit card as its cover. By the midfifties, the number of services and places honoring the card was so large and the book so thick that we issued, for the first time, a separate credit card. By the end of the decade, we had regional booklets for the United States and individual listings for foreign countries. The card continued to made of cardboard until the advent of plastic in the sixties.

We kept pressing to widen the services. Mail order, particularly through the pages of the *Diners Club Magazine* and inserts with the bills, became an important factor. By 1959, you could charge not only for dining and hotel rooms and flowers, auto rentals and airlines, but for liquor and travel insurance and auto supplies, luggage, smoked turkeys, office furniture, and fine cigars.

Impresario Mike Todd was about to premiere his film, *Around the World in Eighty Days*, which would win the Academy Award for 1956. We met and worked out the first charge for movie tickets or for that matter, any entertainment attraction.

Al Bloomingdale was an old friend of Hall-of-Fame slugger Hank Greenberg, who had been married to a cousin of Al's, one of the Gimbel department store clan. Greenberg was, in the late fifties, general manager of the

Cleveland Indians. I asked Al to set up a meeting for me with Hank who then arranged for me to speak at the winter meeting of the baseball owners. I pitched them on honoring the Diners Club card at all big-league ball parks. Greenberg followed me with an enthusiastic endorsement of the project. Then, Frank Lane, who was general manager of the Chicago White Sox, rose from his seat.

"Baseball is America," he said. "Baseball is peanuts and Cracker Jacks—and cash. Using a credit card will slow up the turnstiles and give our sport a feeling of business instead of entertainment." He fingered a sample credit card I had distributed. "This," he said, "is a fad. Just another gimmick the public has gotten hot and bothered about. And it's business—not apple pie. It won't last."

The owners voted against the proposal.

Today, of course, credit cards are honored at nearly all ball parks, at movie houses, on Broadway, and at theaters everywhere.

Credit checks continued to be stringent. Certain industries were considered particularly high risk, and applicants from those industries had to be reviewed by Joe Titus or his closest aides. Riskiest of all were entertainers, and most were simply rejected. They had a tendency to be itinerant and to have a high disregard for paying bills. Sammy Davis, Jr., however, was quickly approved when he applied. He was one of the highest-paid nightclub acts in the world in the fifties and was also appearing in Broadway musicals and in films. Within a year after he got his Diners Club card, he owed twenty-six thousand dollars and wasn't paying.

We wanted to avoid the newspaper publicity that would be attendant to any lawsuit. He was appearing at the Copacabana in New York. Joe and I met with Jules Podell, the gnarly proprietor of what was then America's best-known nightclub.

Podell was a no-nonsense guy. He didn't tolerate trouble, and he considered anything or anyone at his club to be his responsibility. Only a month earlier, I had been seated with friends at a table at the Copa when suddenly we noticed that there wasn't a waiter or head-waiter on the huge floor. For fifteen minutes more than 500 customers sat without help while, in the kitchen, Podell held a meeting at which he alternately ranted and cursed about some inefficiency he had spotted.

Now he left Titus and me alone in his office. We sat there for more than twenty minutes. Finally, Podell, a squat man with the carriage of a large ape, lumbered into the room. He sat down and faced us.

"We worked it out," he said in his hoarse, growl of a voice. "Sammy apologizes. He had some pressing debts." He sighed. "But he's all right now." He reached into his jacket pocket, pulled out an envelope, and handed it to Titus. "Here's your twenty-six thousand dollars. We're gonna work it out with Sammy." It was the easiest collection—and the biggest—to date. We shook hands and left. I learned later that the money was to be deducted from Sammy's Copa salary. Jules Podell didn't like problems.

Schneider and Bloomingdale were as unlikely a pair as Schneider and MacNamara had been. Al was born into an enormously wealthy and famous family. Bloomingdale's, which his family had founded but no longer owned, was a legendary department store. Until the Diners Club, however, he was known for his liaisons with beautiful women and for his personal business failures.

For a while he'd been a Broadway producer. One show he produced was called *Allah Be Praised*. Before its planned opening on Broadway, it settled in Philadelphia for a tryout, and Al, knowing that he had problems, called Cy Howard, a noted comedy writer, to see if he could offer some advice. Howard sat in the audience and watched the show then walked slowly up the aisle as the crowd somberly filed out. Bloomingdale met him in the lobby. "Cy," he beseeched, "what do you think I should do?"

Howard studied him for a moment. "Close the show," he suggested, "and keep the store open nights."

The story has been retold so often that both George S. Kaufman and Groucho Marx have often been erroneously credited with the advice.

Al and his family still owned the enormously valuable land on which the New York Bloomingdale's sat, as well as a large area around it. This led to a much-heard gag at the time. "When Al was kid, his father gave him blocks to play with—Fifty-eighth Street, Fifty-ninth Street...."

Now, for the first time, Al was a success at something other than being born rich. He was president of this new phenomena, and his warm personality and wide range of friends opened many doors. Everybody liked him.

That included Schneider who thought he was a terrific guy but lived in fear of his crackpot ideas and his compulsion to make deals—good and bad. "My principal responsibility in this company," he would often say, "is to see that Al Bloomingdale doesn't destroy us." It was, of course, an overstatement. Al frequently came up with good ideas as well as many that were quickly dismissed. "Oh, well," Bloomingdale would say after one of his plans was shot down, "on to the next one."

He did do a lot of things that helped the enormous growth the company enjoyed in the latter years of the 1950s. One of these was the hiring of a young direct-mail expert named Spencer Nilson. I had created and directed mail solicitations in the early years, but I had more than I could handle. Nilson was brought in and direct mail soon overtook take-one boxes and was again the principal source of new members.

Schneider kept a tight hold on the reins. Once he stormed into my office to complain about something. It was the only time he'd ever raised his voice to me, and I didn't like it. When he left, I sat for a few minutes and smoldered. Then, I charged into his office.

"Who the hell do you think you are?" I yelled. "God?!!"

"In this company," he said softly, "I *am* God."

I was stunned. "I quit!" I snapped and I turned and stomped out.

About five minutes later, he returned to my office. Now, he was smiling. "Where," he asked slowly, "do you want to go to lunch?"

The incident was never discussed again.

Annual domestic charge volume by the end of the decade was closing in on the half-*billion* mark.

The New York and Los Angeles offices had duplicate billing and credit operations. In the early years when the company was borrowing money from factors, before banks thought it was loan-worthy, checks for eastern establishments were drawn out of Los Angeles and for western establishments out of New York. This meant that when a Boston restaurant deposited its monthly check from the Diners Club in its Boston bank, there was a delay of at least three days before that money was paid by our Los Angeles bank—a huge savings in interest rates.

Joe Tilem, who much later became the mayor of Beverly Hills, was head of legal operations at Diners Club-West in Los Angeles during the fifties. He recalls having a huge map of the United States with red pins in it, marking where cardholders who had left their hometowns to avoid paying their bills had been traced to. "How primitive we were then," he said to me in a recent conversation. "I remember we had one guy we chased all over the map. Finally, we got him right in our own city, Los Angeles. He owed us something like six thousand dollars. We grabbed his car and sealed off his hotel room. He showed up at our offices the next day driving a flatbed, then he deposited about twelve large cakes of ice on the sidewalk. Frozen in them were six thousand one-dollar bills."

Tilem went on to become a Carte Blanche vice-president after he left the Diners Club. He's credited with having created the warning bulletin which had the names of accounts whose card should not be honored by member establishments. He remembers the early days with wonder. "Back then," he recalls, "we often had trouble getting a cop to arrest a fraudulent cardholder. Now, it's a federal offense, and the Secret

Service pursues credit-card counterfeiters or thieves like they do guys who print their own money. The credit card," he muses, "has been elevated to the level of currency." Tilem also conceived the idea of insuring cardholders against fraud on lost and stolen cards.

That's what we were doing in the credit-card business in the 1950s—coming up with ideas. We were in a business no one had ever been in before, so there were no guidelines and few limitations. We couldn't hire experts because there were no experts where there had been no business.

People like Dick Kirkpatrick, who retired in the early 1960s and died a year or so later, Joe Titus, and Joe Tilem, for the most part, created the billing and credit operations which would serve until computers took over in the midsixties. I, with much help from Bill Richman, who died of a heart attack in the 1970s, and Spence Nilson, kind of blindly, mostly by instinct, figured out how to sell a credit card to people and how to get businesses to agree to honor that credit card.

The 1950s was a wonderful time for us. We were leading the league every year.

Credit-card issuance was still a measured practice. Cards were not yet given to college and high-school kids, to dogs, or to people on the verge of bankruptcy. That was to come, not with the emergence of American Express as a credit-card superpower, but some years later with the advent of the bank card. The Diners Club was created as a service. We urged people to spend within their means. With no interest on delinquent accounts over thirty days, we wanted people to pay up in a hurry.

All that was to change.

But before it did, starting in 1958, but really heating up in the early sixties, was the first of the two great credit-card wars.

Chapter Five

AMERICAN EXPRESS, THE "FIRST" COMPETITOR

THE COMPANY THAT would become American Express was born in 1841, 109 years before the Diners Club. America was a new, vibrant country with frontiers constantly moving westward, and the population, most of whom were coming in from Europe, moved right out behind the pioneers who reached those frontiers.

Like Frank MacNamara, Henry Wells had an idea. He lived in Buffalo, New York, then a westerly city. People are spreading out, he reasoned, and they'll need deliveries. Packages and cash and papers and gold and silver will have to be ferried from one city to another. This was no simple job: a horse-drawn wagon took four days to travel from Buffalo to Albany. Wells took on mail and charged six cents to transport a letter, whereas the government mail service charged twenty-five. Within four years, his business was so successful, he forced the government to lower its mail delivery rate to two cents, a price that would remain well into the twentieth century.

In 1850, Wells merged his company with his two major competitors, Livingston and Fargo and Butterfield, Wasson and Company. They would dominate what was commonly known as the express business. Henry Wells was chosen president of the new entity which was named American Express.

By 1852, the company was in business as far west as Missouri. Wells and his vice-president, William Fargo, wanted to move on and expand to California where the gold rush had opened new towns and was now attracting farmers and enterprising businessmen.

The board of directors thought the company was expanding too quickly but had no objection to the two men setting up their own stagecoach and express routes in the western United States. The result was Wells, Fargo and Company. Another offshoot would be the Overland Express, a part of which would be the legendary Pony Express, actually a minor dot in American history that has been romanticized in films and books and, of course, in the Wild West magazines which were so popular in the country until the middle of the twentieth century. The Pony Express actually operated for only a year, covered far less territory than readers of its history were led to believe, and proved to be inefficient in its only service, which was transporting mail.

But stagecoaches, and then trains, were not inefficient in those days, and American Express flourished.

By 1862, the company had nearly 900 offices and employed more than 1,500 men. By 1891, Wells and William Fargo had left the company, and a new service was introduced, money orders and traveler's checks. Soon, these would be the services to make American Express famous all over the world.

Profits soared. A little more than a half century later, after World War II, Americans started to travel extensively, and they took American Express traveler's cheques with them. Except for fraud, which was controlled tightly by a huge force of security men, it was just about a risk-free business. You sold the cheques at banks or stores or American Express offices everywhere. You gave a small commission to the banks or retailers who primarily handled the cheques as a service to their customers. American Express then held on to the actual money paid for the cheques until the purchaser redeemed them. Sometimes that would take months or years. Sometimes they would never be redeemed. This was called the "float." And the "float" was reinvested or simply kept on hand for operations, expansion, and profits.

It was a fabulous business. Little investment, little risk, big returns. By 1956, American Express had become the world's biggest service company. It had grown even more prodigiously after the war, and that year its chairman, Ralph Reed, could report that traveler's cheque sales alone were $1.6 billion and rising so quickly that they would double in eight years.

But the board of directors of American Express wasn't quite sure that all was well. There was this "credit-card thing" happening. The Diners Club was growing far beyond anyone's expectations and could it be possible that in years to come—certainly not in the near future—people would use credit cards and not traveler's cheques when they left home? Reed himself dismissed the idea, but his chief aides and members of his board wanted to know more. The matter had to be looked into.

Chapter Six

WHAT ARE THEY DOING THERE?

THE MORE HIS board members urged him to further investigate entrance into the credit-card business, the more Ralph Reed resisted. "Too many pitfalls," he told them. "You're issuing a blank check to people who can have the time of their lives and either belly up or disappear. We're in a business virtually without risk. Why stick our necks out?"

But not only were his board of directors talking credit cards, but his two most trusted lieutenants, Howard Clark and Bob Townsend, alternately spoke of the effect credit cards could have on traveler's cheques and their profits. "Look," Clark would say, "the Diners Club is only seven years old and already listed on the New York Stock Exchange and making millions."

"And," Townsend would add, "their growth is phenomenal. They'll have three-quarters-of-a-million members inside of a couple of years."

Finally, Reed told them to seriously investigate the possibility of buying the Diners Club.

The two men met at lunch with Belmont Towbin and Ben Sonnenberg. Towbin was a partner in Unterberg and Towbin, a small but influential Wall Street brokerage firm, and the most dominant outside member of the Diners Club board. Sonnenberg was a widely known public relations man, a wheeler-dealer who did exactly what he was there to do that day, put people together.

The next day, Towbin met with Schneider and Bloomingdale and told them that American Express was interested in buying out their interests (at that point they each owned one-third of the company) and then tendering an offer for the one-third owned by the public. A figure between four and five million dollars had been vaguely mentioned. Schneider wasn't sure. Bloomingdale was all for the deal.

Ralph Schneider was just getting used to money and power and he liked them both. He'd collect a lot of money if the deal was made, but he also knew he'd no longer be "God."

Bloomingdale, on the other hand, didn't have the power anyway. Schneider kept his flare for gambling and odd schemes pretty much under wraps, and since any deal would have him remain as president of the company and Schneider stay as chairman, he'd be, more or less, in the same place he was, only richer.

It seemed odd, perhaps, that this son of an enormously wealthy family with a large annual income from real estate and other family holdings should need money, but Al Bloomingdale had excessive appetites as did his wife, the glamorous Betsy Bloomingdale. They lived in a huge mansion in Holmby Hills, the upside of Beverly Hills, gave extravagant parties, had a half-dozen imported cars, and traveled extensively. Betsy was consistently named one of America's best dressed women and was famous for her investments in French designers. And, of course, Al was a philanderer, always with a mistress or two and a liking for wild—and expensive— soirees with wild and expensive women and many of his famous pals. And, always an easy touch, he constantly loaned money to friends in need, most of whom never bothered to pay him back.

So Al was all for it. Ralph wanted to have a lot of meetings and a lot of conversations with the American Express people before deciding. The point man for Amex was Bob Townsend, and, after weeks of talks, they settled on a deal. As discussed at the original meeting with Towbin and Sonnenberg, American Express would buy out Schneider and Bloomingdale and then tender the public's shares. The payoff for Schneider and Bloomingdale's stock would come to five million. They would be given various incentives in American Express stock in addition. Clark and Townsend were delighted.

Bloomingdale was ecstatic. Schneider was apprehensive but agreed to make the deal.

Ralph Reed thought about it for a week or so, then turned it down. "The price is too high," he told his board. "We're going to look into doing it on our own."

Some of his board members and executives were incredulous: five million for control of a company already showing profits of more than two million dollars a year before taxes, a company with cardholders and management and billing and credit systems in place? There were major arguments. Clark and Townsend in particular urged him to reconsider. But Reed had his way and the Diners Club deal was dropped.

Townsend had become quite friendly with Schneider during the weeks of negotiation, and now he was ready to quit American Express—he'd had it with Ralph Reed. The two men talked of Townsend coming to the Diners Club. He'd be president, Bloomingdale would be bumped to vice-chairman. Schneider had one small obstacle to clear before making such a deal—me.

Between marketing the club, publishing the magazine which had become an invaluable and highly profitable tool, and closing most of the important contracts for member charge facilities, I had always been the company's key man. I was in no mood to tolerate someone new coming in over me. Schneider asked me what I thought of his idea to bring Townsend into the Diners Club.

"You put in a new man as president," I said coldly, "and I walk."

That was that. Townsend stayed at American Express. A few years later, he became the president of Avis Rent-a-Car and did a brilliant job in that company's formidable challenge to Hertz.

Even though it was announced that Diners Club/American Express discussions had ended, the Diners Club stock took off. Within a year, the market value of the company's shares reached fifteen million dollars. Profits and membership kept pace. We bought out Trip-Charge and the Esquire Club and started negotiations to purchase the card-holding membership of the Sheraton Hotel credit system.

During this time, American Express was girding itself for its entrance into the credit-card business.

Pete Bradford, an American Express senior vice-president, had been most influential in convincing Reed to turn down the Diners Club acquisition. "I am *very lukewarm* on this deal," he wrote in a memo. He had gone on to suggest that it would be wiser and cheaper to start from scratch.

Clark was appointed to head a committee to investigate "how-to" and "how-much" to start an American Express credit card. As the investigation went on, it became apparent that it would have been wiser to acquire the Diners Club.

Ralph Schneider always made a point of keeping Al Bloomingdale out of any negotiations. Al was so anxious to make a deal—any deal—that often you'd discover while hammering out an acquisition or any other major transaction, that you were actually negotiating not only with the people on the other side of the table but with Bloomingdale, whose favorite expression at such tradings was, "Oh, what's the difference? Give them what they want."

So Al moved again, on his own. He contacted an old friend, Gus Levy, the senior partner of the venerable firm Goldman, Sachs and one of the grand patriarchs of Wall Street. He urged him to set up a meeting with Reed to rekindle merger discussions. They met in Reed's office, Bob Townsend was the only other person present. Bloomingdale in his usual florid style went on and on about the potential of an American Express-Diners Club merger.

When they left, Reed wondered, "Why is he so anxious to make this deal? If things are so great and prospects are so glowing, why does he want to work for us?" But Bloomingdale had done one thing. He'd convinced Reed that the future of the credit card was enormous.

Less than a week later, Ralph Schneider, who still hadn't heard about the latest discussions, spoke before the New York Society of Securities Analysts and confirmed the enthusiastic picture Bloomingdale had painted for Reed. Membership, he revealed, was more than 500,000. Billings were surging. Credit losses were minimal.

Within a week, the stock soared to forty-one. The deal once discussed at five million dollars would now have to cost more than twenty million dollars in American Express stock.

Reed and his board agreed, once again, that an acquisition wasn't doable at that price. Howard Clark and Bob Townsend, who had urged that the deal be made a year earlier at one-fourth the price, said nothing.

The recommendation of the board was, "Keep looking into our going into the credit-card business."

Chapter Seven

THEY'RE OFF!

ON OCTOBER 1, 1958, American Express, with $688 million in assets and 108 years of company history behind it, entered the credit-card field. At that point, the Diners Club had enjoyed eight years of success without any real problems other than the one of being able to exist at the very outset which was cured by charging for the card. We'd started as a little business and had succeeded with a lot of luck, a lot of guessing right, and a dollop of the smarts. What we'd always had was confidence. I had personally been against the proposed deal with American Express. I was Schneider's closest friend and confidante, and I had beseeched him not to become part of a huge company. "We're having fun," I would tell him. "We're not gonna have fun as a division of American Express." Despite Bloomingdale's urgings, Schneider had vacillated. Sometimes he favored the buyout, being a major shareholder in American Express, but more often he agreed with me. After all, *now* he was the boss. He answered to no one.

When the American Express announcement that they would offer their own credit card boomed onto the business pages, I remained totally confident. Schneider was wary. "This isn't Trip-Charge or the Esquire Club," he'd remind me. Bloomingdale was worried as hell.

We planned a major mail and advertising campaign to break at the same time as the Amex entrance into the field. Spence Nilson would hit with one million solicitations through the mail, more than double anything we'd ever done before. American Express membership invitations were mailed in early October—eight million of them.

We doubled our sales staff, sharply increasing the number of take-one boxes holding Diners Club applications. We opened displays at rail and air terminals and, for the first time, developed a corporate sales staff; salesmen who would pitch company membership to large—and small—corporations.

Whatever we did, Amex did the same, only with more money and manpower. We had pioneered the field, learning by trial and error what to do and what not to do. They had someone they could learn from—us.

They made only two changes in our service before presenting it to the public and to potential establishments. They lowered the commission paid by those establishments from 7 to 6 percent and increased the annual membership from five to six dollars. They acquired the Gourmet Club credit card, a small offshoot of *Gourmet* magazine, which immediately gave them one thousand member establishments. But getting member establishments was at this point comparatively easy. Eighty percent of those places honoring the Diners Club card would now welcome both.

The official advertised announcement to the public came on October 1, 1958, in the form of full-page ads in America's twenty-three largest newspapers. We responded with our own advertisements in six major papers.

Where we always had the edge was in publicity. Don Simmons's firm had become one of New York's most important press agencies, representing hotels and restaurants and nightclubs, including the Copacabana, and key members of the press were wined and dined regularly. Between us, we'd cook up stunts and stories that gave us free space to match our competitor's advertising dollars.

We started getting reports that our take-one displays in restaurants were disappearing and being replaced by American Express boxes. I phoned Amex's head of marketing and called him on it. He apologized, blaming it on overzealous field men and promised it would stop. Bill Richman, not one to turn the other cheek, had his men go on a two-week demolition campaign, destroying something like ten thousand American Express take-ones before I put a halt to it.

Things were heating up. "See," I reminded Schneider, "this is more fun than ever."

We were street fighters. We were not necessarily smarter, but we were slicker and more daring and knew what would work and what wouldn't. But they did have some enormous advantages: they had a relationship with banks all over the world that sold their traveler's cheques, and those banks gave them displays and invaluable mailing lists of people who traveled. They had their travel agency offices with the obvious contact with consumers who were the most needful of credit cards and, because of their huge profits and the incredible "float" from traveler's cheques, they had cash, endless amounts of it, to pump into this new business. And they could afford to lose money—lots of it—and did for years.

They just kept pouring it on: a nationwide radio campaign, major magazine advertising, and, eventually, television. They spent more on advertising in their first full year in the credit-card business than we had in our entire history.

The drive was on, as well, to sign member establishments to exclusive contracts. If we signed a leading men's clothing chain, they'd follow with that chain's biggest competitor. When they signed Brentano's popular bookstores, we immediately made a deal with Doubleday.

Our edge was that we had more cardholders and could promise and deliver more business. We continued to use the *Diners Club Magazine* as a tool to get establishments and services of every kind. Soon, Amex realized that the magazine was invaluable and decided to create their own.

When they applied for second-class postage which would give them drastically lower rates and faster service than third-class mail (first class is too costly for a magazine), the post office told them they'd have to have a positive request for magazine subscription fees. This meant that instead of having to indicate that they didn't want to subscribe to the magazine, their cardholders would have to request the subscription.

The *Diners Club Magazine*, of course, had both a negative requirement and a second-class permit. American Express officials were quick to point this out. With monthly circulation rapidly approaching one million, we were talking about anywhere from six to eight million dollars a year in additional postal costs should we lose our second-class permit. We hired a lobbyist (a former post-office lawyer), and I was summoned to Washington.

After months of wrangling, the post office decided that since we'd had a second-class permit for eight years, they'd "grandfather" us in. That is, they'd allow us to retain our status, but that any new such requests had to follow the rules. That meant American Express. They hired their own lobbyists who got nowhere, and they were forced to settle for publishing a magazine with a required positive request. The membership paid their card fee, but for the most part did not opt for the magazine. With low circulation, the magazine never took off.

The remaining jewels for the two battling credit-card companies in the hotel and restaurant industry were the Sheraton and Hilton chains which dominated the fields.

Schneider and Bloomingdale had initially met with Conrad Hilton's son, Barron, and several of his associates to discuss turning over the nearly one million Hilton hotel credit cardholders to the Diners Club and converting as many as possible (many would be duplications) to Diners membership.

Diners offered to identify all such cardholders as Hilton-Diners Club members on their credit cards and to conduct a major advertising and promotional campaign to all Diners Club members on behalf of Hilton. The move would have relieved Hilton of enormous bookkeeping and collection expenses. For the conversion, Hilton expected a substantial holding in the Diners Club.

Schneider and Bloomingdale talked about 8 to 10 percent of the outstanding stock. Al, of course, opting for the high end with Ralph protesting all the way. Barron Hilton threatened that Hilton was prepared to go into the credit-card business on its own and compete with both Diners and American Express. He asked for a 20 percent interest in the company. Without even looking at Bloomingdale, Schneider reached out his hand, thanked Hilton and his colleagues for meeting with them, and told them they were too far apart for further discussion. He and a pale Al Bloomingdale walked out of the room.

Two days later, Hilton announced that they were going to compete with Diners Club and American Express. Two weeks after that, Schneider and I met with the top brass at the Sheraton Hotel central office in Boston. Sheraton had already started to form the Sheraton Central Credit Card which was to be a paid membership club, again with plans to compete in the all-purpose credit-card business. They had in place 800,000 customers who held free credit cards. Sheraton had more hotels than Hilton, but they weren't as prestigious as many of the Hiltons, which included the formidable Waldorf-Astoria in New York, probably the world's most famous hotel.

But if Hilton was indeed going into the credit-card business, it meant that they weren't going to sign with American Express either. A deal with Sheraton would not only one-up Amex but offset any Hilton card which would, naturally offer their own hotels.

Sheraton was given everything promised to Hilton and 156,250 shares of Diners Club stock—then worth about five million dollars and representing 12 1/2 percent of the outstanding shares. In addition, Sheraton was given warrants to buy 183,750 more shares at prices ranging from $40 to $43.81. Diners took over Sheraton Central and its 800,000 cardholders and all Sheraton charge operations. Sheraton also agreed to produce at least 200,000 new Diners Club-Sheraton cardholders within a year or pay a penalty of five dollars for each one it fell short.

The usual Diners Club hotel commission—seven percent of net billings—was changed to 4 1/2 percent of gross which meant that for the first time, the Diners Club would be receiving a percentage of such previously uncommissioned items as telephone calls, tips, valet and laundry service, and even, tax. The result was equivalent to a net commission of about six percent and meant bigger tabs and considerably less bookkeeping in that precomputer age.

We quickly followed the huge burst of publicity that ensued with an advertising campaign that revealed very clearly that we had the Sheraton Hotels and Amex didn't. Because of the new credit-card furor, Diners Club membership had risen sharply after American Express' entry into the field and now soared even higher.

We were to find that the number of duplications with Diners Club membership on Sheraton's list was about 40 percent, more than had been anticipated. Also, Sheraton fell short by half on its guarantee to produce 200,000 new Diners Club members within a year and had to fork over $500,000, but it was considered a battle won in the war of the credit-card companies.

"When we made the deal, Sheraton had forty-seven hotels," Schneider would rationalize to *Time* magazine at year-end 1959. "Now, they have fifty-four. We're ahead of the game already."

By January 1, 1960, the Diners Club had 1.1 million members in the United States and almost as many in foreign franchises. In less than two years, American Express had recruited 700,000 paid members. Hilton, now in the all-purpose credit-card business with a card they called Carte Blanche—which was called everything from "Carta Blanka" to "Casablanca" by most of the public—claimed 1 million cardholders, but it was unclear as to how many actually paid for or even asked for the card. And their billings were far lower than their competitors.

Diners Club was clearly still number one, but American Express' growth was prodigious. Despite continuing losses in the credit-card operation, Amex plowed millions into promotion. There was talk again of Amex merging with Diners Club, this time in reverse, with Diners Club taking over the American Express card for a holding of perhaps 20 to 25 percent of Diners. Bob Townsend, who had not yet left Amex for Avis, was in favor of such a move. He'd thought about it carefully. The credit-card venture had indeed dug deeply into the profits generated by traveler's cheques, money orders, and travel agencies.

What happened that had not been anticipated was that in the frenzy to get more cardholders, Amex had set lower credit standards, and Diners Club, battling for numbers and dominance, had followed suit. Diners Club credit losses, once 1/4 of 1 percent, then 1/2 of 1 percent, had now passed 3/4 of 1 percent and was climbing to the 1 percent mark. American Express' losses, not divulged in full to the public at that time (it was an over-the-counter stock and as such was not required to break down intracorporate losses), were known to be substantially more than one percent.

Howard Clark, who chaired the American Express credit-card management committee, made two moves to head off the losses and stop the talk of merging with Diners Club—this time he felt his company had begun something and had to continue. He appointed George Waters to head the credit-card division—Waters would do the job—and he raised the annual credit-card fees to eight dollars. Diners Club followed soon after, charging eight dollars for membership plus two dollars for the *Diners Club Magazine.*

The fee increase would cover the rising credit losses for both companies. At the Diners Club, Joe Titus, for one, wasn't happy. He had been ordered to make the card more available to people in lower-income brackets than we'd established from the very beginning. He argued against it.

"It's wrong," he said at a management meeting one day. "We're giving a blank check to men and women who won't be able to control their spending and will wind up in heavy debt and in court and eventual bankruptcy. It's bad business for us, and it's not fair to them even if they beg us for the damn card."

Schneider wasn't that altruistic. "Our profits are increasing," he said, "even if bad debts are going up." He echoed a pitch I'd given the press for years but that I didn't really believe in myself. "Someday everybody will carry a credit card."

"I hope not," Titus answered. "We'll need a collection department bigger than the U.S. Army if they do."

In addition to cardholders who simply couldn't pay their bills, credit-card thefts, counterfeiting, and fraud started to escalate. Thieves, who since the creation of civilization had come up with new ways to rob others of their valuables and their money, now learned how to steal credit cards. They discovered how to falsify their credit applications so they could get their own cards and copy them much like the counterfeiter mastered the art of re-creating twenty-dollar bills.

But most losses came because of lower standards at the credit department level. As Joe Titus constantly moaned, "Cards are being given to the wrong people."

The most famous "wrong" person was Joseph Robert Miraglia—a nineteen-year-old New York office clerk.

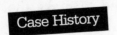

NUMBER ONE

JOE—THE LEGEND

In late August of 1959, Joseph Miraglia was waiting for a friend on a New York street corner when it started to rain. He stepped into the outer lobby of a nearby restaurant to stay dry. It was a good restaurant—one that Joe Miraglia had heard about from fellow workers who could afford to eat there occasionally. On a salary of seventy-three dollars a week, he couldn't.

As he stood there, he was fascinated by three boxes. They held applications for Diners Club, American Express, and Carte Blanche credit cards. He stood looking at them for a while, then he took one application from each box. He later filled out each one and mailed them. Not even a stamp was required for a prepaid envelope came with the application.

Weeks later, he opened the mailbox of his parent's four-room, tenement apartment on New York's East Side where he lived. He had already received letters from the Diners Club and American Express inviting him to reapply when his income, which he'd accurately noted, increased. This time the envelope was from Hilton's Carte Blanche, and it was thicker than the others. This was no letter of rejection. The package contained a handsome Carte Blanche card. Joe walked up the four flights to his apartment, locked himself in his room, put the card on a pillow, and gazed at it for a very long time.

Then he leafed through the booklet that came with it, listing thousands of restaurants and hotels and stores, and it boggled his senses. He could now go to all of these places with the magic card. He reread the letter that came in the envelope. Nowhere did it suggest that he shouldn't use it. Indeed, it said quite clearly, "Joseph R. Miraglia, this card is your key to every luxury Hilton has to offer."

Finally, on the evening of September 10, 1959, he checked into a suite at the Waldorf-Astoria Hotel and immediately ordered two bottles of champagne to be sent to his room. That night he luxuriated in the huge bathtub as he sipped his champagne. The next morning, he ordered room service, then checked out, paying with his new credit card. At the desk they treated him as a special guest, gratefully accepting the card for payment.

He got into a cab and drove directly to the airport. There he charged a ticket to Montreal as he had done in his dreams.

In Montreal, he checked into the luxurious Reine Elizabeth Hotel and again asked for a suite with two bedrooms, two baths, and two television sets. He used them all. Later in the day, he went to the bar and ordered a bottle of their best imported champagne.

This attracted a beautiful blonde. When the new friends finished the champagne, they went to dinner. More champagne and vichyssoise, beef in wine sauce, and crepe suzette. It was a glorious night, even better than his dreams. The next day, the couple visited the fur salon in the hotel where he bought her a silver mink stole and charged it to his room. The woman kissed him goodbye and left.

Before leaving town, he charged a cocker spaniel and a traveling kennel, then went back to New York for a brief stopover before flying on to Las Vegas. At the dice table at the Desert Inn, he stood behind Frank Sinatra while the singer gambled. Finally, Frank turned to him, handed him the dice, and said, "Here kid. You toss 'em." Joe had never had the imagination to dream this well.

Now, he really got into it. Ten-dollar tips to waitresses for bringing him a drink. Another suite and more shopping. And always the card paid for everything.

Two days later, he mulled over his next adventure and decided to again return to New York in the style he had suddenly become accustomed to.

Once there, he checked into a suite at the Plaza, then walked into the Custom Shirt Shop on Fifty-seventh Street, and, flashing his Carte Blanche card, bought eight silk shirts. He walked down Fifth Avenue and spent two thousand dollars on shoes, a Rex Harrison hat, three pairs of silk pajamas, a silver-tipped walking cane, a gray smoking jacket, and fancy luggage. Everything was charged and delivered to his suite.

A few days later, he decided to go to Miami Beach, where people of means went in 1959. He checked into the Fontainebleau, the resort city's premier hotel. Sitting in his suite a few hours later, the credit manager called. A slight problem. He apparently had gone over the credit limit on his Carte Blanche card. Would he mind paying his hotel bill with a check when he left? No hurry, this happens all the time. No reflection on his credit rating. All these cards have limits, you know. Three days later, he wrote a check and left for nearby Havana. It took two bellman to carry his luggage to a waiting taxi.

In Cuba, he checked into the Havana Hilton where he was welcomed and once again told he couldn't use the card. Since he was a valued Carte Blanche member who had merely gone over the standard charge limit, he could pay by check. Of course, he would, knowing what he had known when he'd written the earlier check; his checking account held either ten or twelve dollars. He couldn't remember which. Again, he met a girl and buying her presents and champagne and paying his hotel bill meant that he cashed more than one thousand dollars in checks during his three-day stay in Cuba.

He flew back to New York with the dog, even more luggage, and forty cents in his pocket. He returned to the Plaza, and there it all ended. His checks had started bouncing everywhere. All in all, he'd charged more than ten thousand dollars on his Carte Blanche card and cashed more than two thousand dollars in bad checks.

Considering that he had paid an average of one hundred dollars a day for suites in the best hotels and that those suites at the very same hotels would cost six or eight hundred dollars a day thirty-five or so years later, one could assume that his less-than-three-week "dream trip" today would cost somewhere around sixty thousand dollars.

At the Plaza, two plainclothes detectives showed up at the credit office and arrested him. Overnight, he became a media hero. He'd done what any poor nineteen year old might have done if given the opportunity and the wherewithal. He'd truly had "carte blanche." All he had left now were the dog and his memories and fame. Charges were dropped, and he returned the merchandise. *Time* and *Newsweek* did stories on him, and *Life* magazine paid him to write a first-person account of his adventure. He was, as Andy Warhol might have suggested, "famous for fifteen minutes."

According to a report in a 1991 issue of *New York* magazine, Joseph R. Miraglia did not surface again publicly until 1984, when he was arrested as part of a gang that had counterfeited bank credit cards and sold them to people who went on Miraglia-like spending sprees. This time the money involved was an estimated fifty million dollars.

Now forty-four years old, he was convicted and served a year and a half in a federal prison. His lawyer told me he doesn't know where Miraglia is today.

The spree brought the adventure of the card to the front pages. By 1960, with the banks now issuing cards and the Diners Club and American Express constantly expanding and Carte Blanche sort of bringing up the rear, the country became credit-card crazy.

Where would it end?

The Miraglia story had gotten me thinking, too. Certainly, his being sent a card had been a dumb mistake by someone in the Carte Blanche credit department. He was a nineteen year old making seventy-three dollars a week, living with his parents, no savings account, and a few dollars in a checking account. Whoever issued the card was either asleep on the job or disliked his employers. Did it mean that the original idea of the credit-card business—a system of issuing credit for convenience to established business people— was out the window? In the rush to get more members, would cards be given to people only with dreams and no real way of paying for those dreams?

And now, banks were offering credit cards with time payments: live it up and pay for it whenever.

Would this be an open invitation to disaster? I started to seriously consider what Joe Titus had been so worried about.

One more time, Schneider and Bloomingdale and Clark, who had now replaced Reed as president of American Express, were brought to the negotiating table by Belmont Towbin. By early 1961, American Express was still losing millions in the credit-card business, and Diners Club, although its U.S. membership would move past 1.25 million, had seen, for the first time, a slowdown in the acquisition of new members.

Annual volume crept up slowly, but the slowdown in growth was alarming. Bloomingdale urged a sale to Amex or a merger or acquisition of their credit-card holdings for an even-greater slice of Diners than had been discussed earlier. An outright cash purchase of Diners Club stock now carrying a huge price tag might have been an easy deal in the acquisition-happy days of the 1980s but was considered too much of a gamble in the sixties. An acquisition in stock by Amex would have surrendered more shares than they were prepared to give.

The Amex board weighed the possible sale of their credit-card system. For the first time, a majority of the board leaned toward it. They weren't used to red ink on American Express' ledgers and despaired over it. But this time, Clark was against it.

Mike Lively, one of Clark's trusted lieutenants at the time, recalled the meetings with Schneider and Bloomingdale in an interview some years later. "They came out with a big bluff about how successful they were," he told a writer, "and how unsuccessful we were, and how stupid it was for us to come out with a plastic card [instead of cardboard]—a *dumb* thing to do, nobody wants to use a plastic card, you've got to have *their* kind of system. *They* have all the experts. *They* really know the business. *We* were struggling."

Lively's recollection of the dialogue at meetings between the two companies may have been accurate, but I doubt it. Hyperbole like that fitted the style of neither Schneider nor Bloomingdale. Ralph was not one for either hard sell or tearing the other guy down. Bloomingdale was simply too sweet a person and too anxious to make a deal to risk offending anyone. Furthermore, Schneider confided in me and described every aspect of the talks, and no such references were in those descriptions.

The plastic card, like computerized billing, was something we all knew would come, but it had to come with imprinters, and Amex simply moved more quickly with all these new facets of the business than did Diners Club. Amex stayed in the credit-card business. There would never again be talks between the two companies.

The war resumed.

Chapter Eight

THE

PUBLICITY STUNT

AL BLOOMINGDALE'S mansion in Holmby Hills had, among other things, a huge pool and a tennis court and an electric trolley that transported food from the house down the side of the hill it sat on to a lush picnic area within the grounds of the estate.

The house had been decorated in great splendor by William Haines who, incongruously, had gone from a somewhat-effete cowboy film star to being the interior decorator to the hoi polloi of Los Angeles. In 1962, on one side of the Bloomingdale mansion lived neighbor Frank Sinatra and on the other side, Buddy Adler who was also one of Al's closest friends.

Adler, married to onetime film actress Anita Louise, was the head of Columbia Pictures and one of the most powerful men in the film industry. Al had an idea and Buddy liked it. Why not a movie about this new American phenomenon, the Diners Club?

Between them, they roughed out a story; a lowly clerk at the Diners Club mistakenly issues a credit card to some unsavory people, and for the rest of the movie, he tries to get it back. Studio writers fleshed it out, and Danny Kaye, then a huge star, was cast as *The Man From the Diners Club*.

In New York, we were, of course, delighted. It would be another publicity windfall, timed perfectly to come out as the battle between the two credit-card companies intensified.

When filming on the picture was completed, Charley Powell, head of marketing at Columbia, came to see me. He asked if there was anything special we could do for the movie's world premiere. He wanted something that would create a stir.

A week later I proposed a stunt that I had long dreamed of, something right out of Edward Bellamy's *Looking Backward*. We premiere the film in a small middle-American city. We take over the city for twenty-four hours, issue miniature credit cards to everyone in the city, and, in that one day, no cash is accepted anywhere; not at a grocery store or a car dealer or for a newspaper or a haircut. Not for anything.

In 1963, the Diners Club and American Express credit cards were still basically used for travel and entertainment. The bank cards, still in an experimental stage, had not yet been widely accepted at supermarkets or department stores or for many other daily needs and certainly not for such incidentals as newspapers or magazines or at coffee shops and for other low ticket-purchases. Bellamy's prophecy was to be a reality, at least for one day. All that would be necessary to buy whatever you needed was to possess the one little card.

It took us two months to find the right community willing to make this leap to the future for one day.

Winsted, Connecticut, was perfect—its population was officially documented at 10,496, enough people to fashion an impressive story around and yet small enough to control. Winsted was 125 miles northeast of New York City, close enough to bus press and celebrities there, but far enough that it wasn't considered a New York suburb.

The Winsted city officials were delighted with the opportunity to be the site of a world premiere for a major studio film, and, of course, Danny Kaye would be there. We put on a special staff to supervise the issuance of the credit cards and their acceptance at every retail store and service facility in town. Even the doctors and dentists in Winsted agreed to honor the card, a charge service none of us had even considered until then. At city hall, any parking tickets or other fines paid for on the big day would be charged to the credit card.

Two weeks before the premiere, some sixteen thousand credit cards were issued to the townspeople of Winsted and to those (mostly farmers) who lived in its environs.

Among the places that would honor the card, there was only one holdout—a supermarket which was part of a national chain and couldn't get an okay from its front office because some vice-president had decided it would be against company policy.

Don Simmons, in Winsted preparing for the upcoming press junket for the premiere, would have none of this. He put a call through to the president of the chain, identifying himself as the town mayor. When the call was taken, he explained the problem but was again told that the refusal of cash would violate company policy. Firmly, Don stated that if acquiescence was not forthcoming he—the "mayor"—would personally head a boycott of the store.

"Oh," came the reply, "well, I suppose we could do it this one time."

Six buses were rented to drive press people from New York for the premiere and the charge-only experiment. Limousines would ferry Schneider, the Columbia brass, and, of course, Danny Kaye and his entourage. Every room in the town's only hotel, actually an inn, was rented. Press headquarters was set up at city hall. Diners Club signs and stickers were plastered all over town. A special Diners Club office where cardholders or establishments could call with problems was opened, and for two days, a week before the *day,* Diners representatives once again visited every one of the merchant and services that would honor the card.

Don reported that national magazines, radio, and television news would be in the press caravan. The New York press, however, would not be there.

The premiere was scheduled for March 12, 1963. The previous December, the New York newspapers had gone out on strike and "temporarily" ceased publication. When we had started to plan the premiere, we were assured the strike would end "momentarily." It finally ended on March 31, nineteen days too late for us. With no idea when the strike would end and the picture set to open nationwide only days after the premiere, the event went on.

I arrived in Winsted on March 11. I had already been there several times to meet with the mayor and the city council and with the editors of the *Winsted Citizen.* That evening I wrote what would be a front-page editorial for the paper. It appeared the next morning under a banner headline that screamed in big, bold letters,

CASH DIED TODAY IN WINSTED

"This is an obituary. It's about something that's always been very near and dear to us. It's about something some people have too much of, others have barely enough of and some, who love it fondly, seem to get rid of as soon as they get it. Cash, which was born several thousand years ago, the son of Barter, the adopted child of Trade, died today in Winsted, Connecticut, a small American city on the banks of the Mad River. Cash will be born again tomorrow, but it will never be the same. It may eventually suffer a complete death like the horse and buggy and spats and the kerosene lamp and the zeppelin and the American buffalo.

"Cash died today in Winsted and may eventually die everywhere because it simply didn't keep up with the fast-moving world. Cash simply hasn't become modern.

"The doctors who treated the patient before it died in Winsted came up with the following diagnosis: Why did cash die? It got dirty. It ripped. It faded and people lost it and had no way to claim it if somebody else found it. When you had some of it, somebody was always trying to borrow some from you. When you used it, you had to stop and count it and examine it, and so did the person you gave it to. Sometimes it was too big for a cab ride and too small for a dinner. It was easily gambled away and carried some ten-odd million germs per bill. It created an unseemly bulge in one's pocket when one had too much of it and a saddening depression when one had too little of it. It was absolutely irre-

placeable when accidentally dropped into the family
incinerator and was something you had to worry about
having too much of when walking down a dark street
and too little of when walking into an expensive store.

"Cash will be missed. People got used to it, but cash
was replaced in Winsted today and may eventually be
replaced everywhere by something else people have
become used to—the credit card.

"The Diners Club, one of cash's most powerful
adversaries since it was born in 1950, was appropriate-
ly enough the chief pallbearer at cash's funeral today.
This day in Winsted saw 10,000 people do all their buying without cash. They used only a Diners Club card.

"For those who will grieve for cash, we are delighted to be able to tell you that its death was painless. The
exact time of that death was 12:01 A.M. March 13th,
Winsted time. The time the modern world caught up
with an elderly system that simply gave way to a simpler, more convenient, and efficient one."

Danny Kaye and other featured players in the film
came to Winsted, and that Saturday evening, the premiere, replete with celebrities, floodlights, and sidewalk radio interviews, went exactly as planned. The
entertainment press doted on the small town getting the
Big-City world-premiere treatment, but most of the
newspeople were there to see how the "cash is dead"
stunt would work. It worked to perfection. People,
including the press who had also been given the one-
day credit cards, charged for everything. All charges
were accepted without a hitch.

Everything went as planned. Well, almost everything. The movie itself was a dud. It opened nationally

on April 24 to less-than-enthusiastic reviews and audience response. Bosley Crowther, the *New York Times* film critic, described it thusly: "Most of this reckless, rootless nonsense has our counterfeit comic (Kaye) racing around in ever-widening circles as though he were playing follow-the-leader with an invisible Jerry Lewis. If the original Mr. Kaye should somewhere read this, we hope he will return and be forgiven."

The press coverage on the credit-card experiment was worldwide. Ralph and I and our wives drove back from Winsted early that Sunday morning. "You know," he said with uncharacteristic optimism, "Edward Bellamy is looking pretty good."

Chapter Nine

THE SIXTIES...
THE BEST...
THE WORST

IN THE LATE 1950S, BankAmericard surfaced. It was intended for people who wanted to buy but who couldn't, or didn't want to, pay in thirty days. This experiment was to founder while its not easily surmountable problems were being solved. Eventually it would lead to Visa and to (Mastercharge) MasterCard.

Meanwhile, the Diners Club was still the "king," but American Express with its almost unlimited resources and manpower was gaining. Howard Clark, after he replaced Ralph Reed in 1960, pledged to make the Amex credit card profitable and to make it the world's number-one charge system.

Now, the giant hotel chains and famous restaurants that had held out could no longer resist the demand of those nearly two million travelers and business people who wanted to use one credit card to charge and get one bill. Between 1960 and 1965, the two credit-card giants would sign the vast Holiday Inn chain, Quality Courts, the exclusive Sherry-Netherland in New York, the Pump Room and the Ambassador East in Chicago, the Mark Hopkins in San Francisco, the Emerald Beach in Nassau, the Tisch brothers' estimable Loew's Hotels, which would include the Americanas in New York and Miami Beach and the new Regency on Manhattan's Park Avenue, and tens of thousands of other fine hotels all over the world.

In the fifties, we used guile and constant sales pitches and delivered free advertising and promotion. In the sixties, it seemed all we had to do was hold out a contract, and another establishment would sign it.

After the domestic airlines agreed to honor the cards, the foreign carriers joined the parade.

Sunoco, Union Oil, and Philips all signed Diners Club and Amex contracts, and the other major chains would not be far behind.

Throughout the fifties, the American Hotel Association, led by Seymour Weiss, president of the classic Roosevelt Hotel in New Orleans, had waged a war against credit cards and the Diners Club in particular. On the brink of issuing its own all-purpose credit card, the association finally sold its list of cardholders to American Express. Soon after, Seymour Weiss himself signed a contract for his hotel to honor Diners Club cards.

Diners Club rates charged to establishments now ranged from the 4 percent off gross paid by airlines to 6 percent and 7 percent of net discounted from restaurant and store charges.

American Express had established a sliding scale which had bottomed out at 3 percent for high-volume and high-dollar purchases. That was nudged up to a 4 percent floor by 1965. Most restaurants still paid 6 percent of net charges.

Amex was still testing, trying new approaches, and introducing new systems. George Waters, who had been in charge of data processing for the air force during World War II, had a plan even before taking over American Express' credit-card operations. He'd analyzed the Diners Club systems and decided that Amex could be more efficient, more effective, and more profitable if it went from a basic hand-billing and processing system to computers.

Now, in the 1960s, he switched American Express over to computer billing and issued the plastic credit card.

If step one had been Frank MacNamara's dream, the next giant step had been taken by Waters.

He one-upped the Diners Club with computers then jolted them with faster payments to the establishments. Diners Club, since its inception, had paid its member establishments in thirty days. Now Amex paid in less than a week, giving itself a huge edge with cash-hungry proprietors.

But Diners Club by 1965 still had the cachet earned from being first and having the most members. Now, tourists and businessmen of all nations were traveling to other countries. Diners Club, because its foreign operations were all franchises owned and operated by nationals in each particular country, had far more cardholder and establishment representation outside the U.S.

But things happened in 1964 that would affect the industry and that would make these the worst years of my life.

On August 19, 1964, I owned a horse racing at Roosevelt Raceway. I'd bought several harness horses, and that night, I drove to the track to watch this particular horse race for the first time. As I walked into the paddock, Art Fisher, whose advertising agency represented the Diners Club, stood waiting for me. His eyes had the look of someone carrying a message he didn't want to deliver. Earlier that evening, as I had driven to the track, my brother Don, sitting at a table in Downey's restaurant, turned to say something to the person facing him, then fell, face down across the table. He died at once.

The loss to me, of course, was indescribable. He was my brother and best friend. He'd been my partner and had brilliantly publicized this new American phenomenon. American Express had poured millions into advertising to convey its message to the public. The Diners Club, fashioned on the MacNamara-Schneider investment of eighteen thousand dollars, obviously could not do that, and publicity, enormous gobs of free press, had been what sold it.

Ralph Schneider sat behind me and my family at my brother's funeral. Less than three months later, on November 3, 1964, as we sat in our private dining room in the Diners Club boardroom, Ralph turned to me and said that he had a terrible back pain. His son Jimmy was working for the company. I called him and told him to take his father home. Then I telephoned Ralph's wife and suggested that she call the family doctor.

Jimmy Schneider phoned me two hours later. Ralph, who had taken Frank MacNamara's brilliant idea and gripping the reins tightly had steered it to where it had become the world's newest industry, had died of a heart attack. Adventurers claim that the romance of business has gone because there are no new frontiers to cross, but Frank MacNamara and Ralph Schneider did cross a new frontier. And now, only fourteen years after introducing the credit card as we know it, they were both gone.

Case History
NUMBER TWO
PHYLLIS—THE YOGURT QUEEN

Phyllis told me that if the credit card had never been invented, she'd be "washing dishes or selling my body if anyone would buy it."

An attractive, bright woman in her early forties, Phyllis left a bad marriage ten years before and came to Chicago "with $180 and a Visa card in my pocketbook. I'd never really had a career. I'd been married twice, worked, worked as the manager of a Baskin-Robbins store, but, mostly, had been a housewife—the kind who sat around waiting for her husband to come home, filling in the day with soap operas and dumb novels and occasional lunches with my girl friends.

"I took a couple of college courses but really didn't find anything I liked. My first husband discouraged my pursuing any kind of career, then he waltzed off with a woman—also married—who was a vice-president of a company he did business with.

"I got some money in the divorce settlement and decided I'd never marry again. Six months later, I met a guy—a pilot for one of the major carriers. He was charming and funny and good looking as hell.

"We got married in Las Vegas three weeks after we met. I think we were both drunker than we should have been. It was the marriage from hell. We argued all the time. He'd get drunk and beat me. I'd get drunk and throw things at him. His schedule was irregular so he didn't want me to work either. He wanted me to be around when he flew back into town. He did get me my own MasterCard.

"In a matter of months, I was fed up. I wasn't going to spend another 'lifetime' in a bad marriage. I moved out; didn't even call him. I just packed my things, took my credit card, a thousand dollars I'd saved, and moved into a one-bedroom apartment in Milwaukee which was the biggest city near to us.

"That's when I worked as the manager of Baskin-Robbins for a while—hardly a career—then I decided to go to Chicago.

"I moved in with a girl friend, and in six months I was down to $180. I tried to get a job, but either I wasn't right for them or they weren't right for me. Then, one day I saw this empty store.

"I stood out front and looked at it for a long time, then I decided to rent it. And I had $180. I walked around for a while. What was I going to do with a store? What could I sell? The only thing I knew even a little about was ice cream, and I had just about no money.

"Then I remembered the credit card. I contacted the real-estate office. They'd rent it to me for twelve hundred a month and wanted first and last month's rent. I filled out an application, putting in all sorts of ridiculously phony information, then I went to a bank and drew out five grand on my credit-card account. My husband had OK'd the card, and I had a pretty high limit.

"I kept filling out all sorts of phony information, using cash from the card, and charging for everything else I could.

"I opened a frozen yogurt shop. I paid back all my debts, including my credit-card bills, in six months.

"I've got three stores now. I also got my divorce. A hundred and eighty bucks and a credit card—that did it.

"I just spent twenty thousand dollars on a trip to Europe. I charged everything—but now I can pay for it."

Chapter Ten

THE

FAT LADY SINGS

RALPH SCHNEIDER'S death meant more than the passing of an era at the Diners Club. He had been a close friend and my mentor. Sixteen years older than me, he had given me stability and confidence in a world I'd never been in before. A publicity man in the entertainment world is more a dreamer than a businessman. I'd learned how to sell a business on the job at the Diners Club under Ralph's stewardship.

But to the company, his death was more than a personal tragedy. It meant Al Bloomingdale, liked by everyone—affable and kind and anxious to do the right thing—was in charge. Al had mastered the art of turning a fortune into a shoestring, and despite the success of the Diners Club, he hadn't lost that knack. Only Schneider had reined in Al's desire to make deals at any price and to sink company money into disastrous schemes. "You run the company," Ralph had told me. "I'll stick around just to keep Al under control."

We met a few days after Ralph died. Al told me that he knew I expected to become president of the company (he had already assumed the chairmanship), but that in meetings with outside members of the board, there was reluctance to give me the job. I knew from the time Ralph Schneider had mentioned bringing Bob Townsend into the company, the idea was Belmont Towbin's. The Wall Street contingent on the Diners board wanted a president with "an image," like Townsend, who had been a major figure with an old, big company. After all, despite my successes at the Diners Club, they still seemed to see me as a hotshot Broadway press agent who had come aboard when the company was too small to afford someone of greater stature.

Al asked me to be patient, not to rock the boat. He promised he would never agree to bring anyone in over me. Meanwhile, he would retain the title of president as well as chairman.

Within a year after Schneider's death, Al, who listened to everybody and who had developed his own cadre of lieutenants, decided that Dick Kirkpatrick, inventor of the billing systems for credit-card companies, should retire. Work began on the conversion to computers. Like American Express, we'd have plastic cards and imprinters and computer billing. The hand-billing system would go.

As soon as word got around about the coming of computers, the clerks in the credit and billing departments decided to strike for job security. For almost a month, the company was chaotic. Wives and children of executives came in to shuffle papers and mail out bills.

When the strike was settled, the changeover to computers began. By 1967 the entire Diners Club billing operation would leave the antiquated world of manual billing and in a state of confusion and ineptness of classical proportions, enter a new era.

Al and I disagreed constantly about new schemes he wanted to introduce including the absorption of the Fugazy Travel Service to form Diners-Fugazy. I didn't think we needed to invest in travel agencies, but Al felt that Amex had travel agencies so we should, too. That deal wasn't made until after I left the company.

It was hard to be angry with him. He was like a big kid. If anyone needed help, he was there with money or kind words. He loved the company and reveled in its success. Now that he was in charge, he no longer thought about merging or selling out to a "big brother."

But the Schneider family, sitting with millions in Diners Club stock that could only be sold in small yearly increments through the stock market, was getting antsy. Ralph's sons, Jimmy and Bobby, had no desire to become corporate executives, and his second wife, Ronnie, simply wanted to cash out and start a new life. Shortly after Ralph's death, Continental Insurance Company purchased the shares owned by the Schneider estate and the stock owned by Sheraton Hotels; a total of 835,254 shares for an estimated purchase price of fourteen million dollars. It now owned 34 percent of the company.

Little by little, outside "experts" were filtered into the company. Joe Titus retired. In 1966, Bloomingdale hired a researcher by the name of Ernest Loen to examine the potential of the credit-card industry. Loen and his people spent months on the project, then reported to us that the future growth of the credit card was limited, with a ceiling of perhaps 1.5 to 1.8 million cardholders being available to Diners Club or American Express, "It was no longer," he declared, "a growth industry."

By 1966, I had decided that it was time for me to go as well. Al asked me to stay until they could bring in marketing and publishing people to replace me. I remained until mid-1967, operating as a lame duck for the last six months.

In 1965, members of the Diners Club board, who were primarily Wall Street investors or stockbrokers (there were four "inside" members—Bloomingdale, financial VP Jules Asch, administrative VP Dave Fry, and me), convinced Al that people were knocking on our door and we should listen. The "people" were two banks, the Westminster Bank of England and the Chase Manhattan Bank of New York, both giants in the world of finance. Westminster was a minority stockholder in the Diners Club of Great Britain. Now they wanted to talk about taking over the entire Diners Club U.S. operation. Westminster settled for buying an even-bigger stake in the British operation.

Talks with Chase Manhattan lasted through most of 1966, ending finally when the Justice Department notified Chase that they would look askance at such a formidable banking institution owning the world's largest credit-card company.

American Express has been mentioned as one possible source of complaint that brought on the government scrutiny as have various other major banks. At any rate, the deal never happened, and J. Victor Heard wasn't happy.

J. Victor was the bearlike chairman of Continental Insurance, a man who radiated wisdom. There was no doubt, when you looked at him, that J. Victor was a smart guy.

He lived in Brooklyn Heights, just across the East River from lower Manhattan where the office from which he ran his now-burgeoning empire was located. Each morning four or five of his younger executives would meet him at the foot of the Brooklyn Bridge, and together they would walk across and into Manhattan and to the Continental office. Some, it was suggested, didn't even live in Brooklyn but arrived at the bridge just to join the walks with their boss.

Those mornings in 1966, they'd talk about the possible Westminster/Chase buyouts of the Diners Club falling through. J. Victor had originally bought the Diners Club stock from the Schneider estate for almost seventeen dollars a share. By 1970, they were selling at ten to twelve dollars. No other buyers had shown up in the two years since the banks bowed out. The stock had dropped after the acquisition talks had ended and never recovered. J. Victor Heard decided he'd have to do something dramatic.

On February 7, 1970, one day short of the twentieth anniversary of the day Frank MacNamara had paid for our lunch with the first all-purpose credit card, Heard announced that the Continental Corporation would acquire the 66 per cent of the Diners Club that they did not already own through a tender offer at $15 a share.

Only six months earlier, at the annual meeting of the credit-card company, Heard, representing his minority ownership, had declared that he had no plans to acquire the rest of the Diners Club. "We have made an investment in the credit-card company, and that is all," he had said.

What had happened from the time Continental had really gone into Diners Club for "an investment"?

Nothing good.

Either of the bank deals or a merger with American Express would have netted Continental a healthy profit. Heard had gambled on that.

By the end of the sixth decade, bank cards had entered the picture, and anybody with any foresight could see that they would be a major factor. American Express with its unlimited cash resources, travel offices, and bank connections had now overtaken the Diners Club. Furthermore, new executives installed by Continental had, combined with the poorly conceived conversion to computers, proven disastrous.

By 1970, American Express had 1.5 million U.S. cardholders. Diners Club had quickly shrunk from a peak of 1.3 million U.S. cardholders to little more than a million. Amex charge volume was, each month, running substantially ahead of Diners, and they had, with no little arrogance, elevated the annual membership fee to fifteen dollars a year—and gotten away with it. The earlier misgivings about charging too much for credit-card membership were down the drain. Diners members still paid eight dollars plus two dollars for the magazine.

After six years of losses, American Express card operations finally showed a profit in 1964. By 1970, those profits were huge; the membership fee itself grossing almost twenty million dollars for the year.

On June 18, of 1970, the Diners Club, still in the process of becoming a Continental subsidiary but with enough stockholders who hadn't yet accepted the Continental offer to require public disclosure, revealed that for the first time in the history of the company, it had lost money; it had lost a lot of money.

Losses after taxes were $23 million. The previous year it had seen record operating revenues of $67,723,000, but a dismal net income of $914,000, a profit many millions less than the company had annually enjoyed almost from its inception.

Company executives explained that the losses had been partly the result of computer problems which had swallowed millions of dollars in charges that were never billed. In addition, the company lost many millions on its investment in Diners Club-Fugazy travel agencies. The *Diners Club Magazine* (*Signature*), once the source of millions in profits, was now floundering and would soon be sold.

The announcement came six months after Al Bloomingdale's resignation as chairman of the company. His original investment of $275,000 had netted him approximately $13 million. For the rest of his life he would, as he told me one day, "tinker."

His friend Ronald Reagan, then governor of California, named him to the commission on highway beautification, one of the many areas in which Al had no expertise. He did invest well in a combination hotel-restaurant-boat-docking operation in Florida called the Marina Bay Club and Hotel which flourished.

He became a board member of Twenty-first Century Communications, the company I started when I had left the Diners Club and which, in 1970, was publishing *Weight Watchers* magazine and the *National Lampoon*, with both showing substantial profits.

By 1981, Reagan, of course, was president, and Al was a member of his "kitchen cabinet," a group of wealthy Californians with strong conservative leanings who had financed Reagan from the start of his political career. Betsy Bloomingdale was Nancy Reagan's confidante and would later be known as the "First Friend."

Al died of cancer on August 20, 1982. Soon after, his relationship with his longtime mistress, Vicki Morgan, became front-page news and television *"Hard Copy"* fodder when she sued his estate for the millions he had supposedly promised her. In the process, his penchant for wild sex became daily reading. In July, 1983, less than a year after Al died, Vicki was beaten to death by a former boyfriend.

In the sixteen years or so Al and I worked together, we'd never exchanged an angry word. I never saw or heard of him doing anything that would harm or deceive anyone in business. His sex life was his own concern. At the Diners Club and for the years after when he would attend my board meetings or we would dine together and reminisce about the early credit-card days, I knew him only as a man with enormous enthusiasm and a weakness for making bad deals.

I was despondent when he died. There had been three of us at that table at Major's Cabin Grill the day that cash died, but there were four of us who had really given birth to the damn thing.

| Case History | **NUMBER THREE**
DAVID—THE LOVER |
| --- | --- |

We'll call him *David. He worked as an assistant to one of the editors of a well-known national magazine in New York. His office was a tiny cubicle in a large midtown office building. He lived with his mother on the upper West Side, loved theater and company softball games, dated casually, lived within his rather frugal means, and had one credit card, a Visa account with which he charged an average of one or two hundred dollars a month, mostly on clothes or gifts or dates at inexpensive midtown restaurants like T.G.I. Fridays or at the Hard Rock Cafe.

One night he stood in the long line at the Hard Rock with a couple of guys from his office. In front of them were two girls. One was dazzling. She had long blonde hair and a full body which was accentuated by the tight tank top and leather skirt she wore. He couldn't take his eyes off her. He struck up a conversation, and *Lisa and her friend joined his group at a table. By the end of the evening, he was in love and falling in love was not a regular occurrence for David who, as has been suggested, was kind of conservative. In a departure from his normal straightforwardness, he told her he was an editor at his magazine. She was impressed, and at the end of the evening, he asked if she'd have dinner with him the next night.

"Where?" she asked.

"Wherever you say," he answered.

"The Four Seasons?" she suggested.

He paled slightly. The Four Seasons was one of New York's finest and most expensive restaurants. On the third night, they had sex, accompanied by champagne and elegant room service, in a suite at the Regency Hotel on Park Avenue. For the next month, they saw each other four or five times a week and always at pricey restaurants or in orchestra seats at hit shows which he started buying at premium prices through brokers.

In large upward steps, his credit-card charges started to approach his charge limit. He called Visa and asked that his three-thousand-dollar limit be raised, and they quickly made it five thousand dollars. Just to be safe, he applied for two other credit cards. He lied about his salary on the applications, increasing it from thirty-four to eighty-four thousand dollars. Actually all he did was smudge the three so it looked like an eight. He listed his job at the magazine as editor.

The good times with Lisa went on. After a trip to Atlantic City in a rented car, he went over his Visa credit limit. The next day he got a new MasterCard with a seven-thousand-dollar limit. He celebrated by taking Lisa to an expensive Chinese restaurant on the upper East Side. The next day he applied for still another card, and then another.

Now, he started buying her gifts. They flew to Cape Cod for a couple of days and then went back to Atlantic City for a weekend, during which he drew more than two thousand dollars in cash which they lost at the gaming tables.

He'd never heard of Joseph Miraglia, the first credit-card celebrity, but he was retracing his steps and not with one card but with four.

He started thinking about marriage, and one evening, he hinted it to Lisa. She suddenly got very quiet, and nothing more was said about it that night.

He had been paying for his charges by sending checks for the minimum amount required. But now things were getting out of hand. It had been five months since he'd started dating Lisa, and now he owed credit-card companies more than twenty-nine thousand dollars, only five thousand dollars less than he earned during the entire year. He stopped giving his mother money for the rent, stopped seeing his friends. He concentrated all his energy on his courtship.

When he missed payments on his credit-card bills, someone from Visa called him. He explained that he'd had an illness in the family but would soon take care of the matter. "We're going to have to have your card," the caller said.

Two days later, he picked out a great sweater for Lisa at a chic Madison Avenue shop. He handed over a MasterCard card. The clerk ran it through the machine that "talks" to the banks. "I'm sorry," she told him, "but we can't accept this card. There's apparently some problem with your account." He walked out briskly, his face flushed.

That night, he and Lisa went to the River Club, a fine restaurant frequented by monied New Yorkers. After a dinner at which she hardly spoke, they drove back to her place. She sat on the couch next to him. "You know, David," she said slowly, "I bought a copy of your magazine today, and in the place where they list the staff, you're down there as an editorial assistant, not the editor."

He stared at her. "I know," he said. "I became an editor six months ago, and we keep forgetting to change the masthead."

She stared at him.

"David," she said, "you're an editorial assistant, and you make around twenty-five thousand dollars year. A friend of mine told me that's about what editorial assistants make."

He sat there and thought about this. "Thirty-four thousand a year," he said. "I make thirty-four thousand a year."

"How can you afford all the restaurants and the gifts and the trips?"

"My family," he said after a pause. "We're very wealthy."

Lisa, although beautiful and vivacious, wasn't the smartest girl in the world, or even the second smartest, but most beautiful and vivacious girls have been on the receiving end of a lot of lies, and they learn to recognize the truth. She grimaced.

"Credit cards!" he blurted out. "Credit cards! And I owe nearly thirty grand."

She leaned over and kissed him, then she turned off the lights, and they took off their clothes, and they made love. When they were finished, he got dressed and she put on a robe and walked him to the door. "Goodbye, David," she said. "It's been great, but I can't see you anymore." He was still numb when he stepped out into the street. He walked the three miles to his mother's apartment.

That week, the rest of his cards were canceled, and a man called from one of the banks and told him that it seemed that he had falsified his credit-card application. "That," the man said, "is a crime. Furthermore, it's a crime to spend more money on a credit card than you can reasonably afford to pay."

That confused David since most of the people he knew spent more money on a credit card than they could reasonably afford to pay. But he didn't argue. He told his mother what he had done. After some major histrionics and some name-calling of a nature he had never before heard come from her lips, she called her brother Stephen who was a lawyer.

Stephen reached a settlement with the credit-card companies. His mother loaned David the money, and he paid off at about fifty cents on the dollar. He is now repaying her out of his salary which was recently increased to thirty-six thousand dollars a year.

Lisa met a man in the liquor business, got married, and moved to New Jersey.

A year or so after the settlement, David applied for another credit card but was rejected. On good nights, when he's had a beer or two, maybe after a softball game, he will admit that those months with Lisa and his credit cards were the best time of his life.

Chapter Eleven

THE BANK
CARD ARRIVES

ARTHUR ROTH WAS a helluva banker. He'd built his Franklin National Bank on Long Island to where it was the most formidable independent banking institution in New York's most heavily populated suburb. In 1951, he was sure about one thing: Frank MacNamara's credit-card scheme was a good one, and he wanted his bank to get in on it.

Before the Diners Club was two years old, Franklin National (later to be renamed the European-American Bank) issued credit cards to customers who were using them at restaurants and stores throughout the Long Island area. Soon after, the First National Bank of San Jose, California, got into the act and offered the same service.

Although they did feature installment or time-payment credit, making them *credit* cards as opposed to Diners Club which was and is in reality a *charge* card, there seemed to be no great enthusiasm for the service.

115

It took nearly seven years for any major bank to get into the credit-card business. On October 1, 1959, the Bank of America, then the country's largest financial institution, launched BankAmericard, announcing, among other things, that it was sending unsolicited credit cards which required no fee to more than one million of its customers. It had, the bank stated, signed contracts with more than twenty-five thousand California restaurants, stores, gas stations, and other businesses that would honor the cards.

Over the next four years, Bank of America lost millions of dollars on bad debts, start-up costs, and poor management.

But, in 1964, they announced that credit-card operations were in the black, that membership which at one point had risen to more than 1.3 million had now settled to just over a million because of "judicious pruning of potential credit risks," that credit limits for cardholders were between $350 and $500 depending on their credit worthiness, and that single purchase limits which had been $50 at the outset of the plan would now be raised to $100.

At the time, banks could only do business in the state in which they were chartered, so all of BankAmericard's cardholders and member establishments were in California. The only way to move out and grow was franchising. And that's what they did.

By 1966, a plan was drawn up by an imaginative vice-president named Kenneth Larkin. Interchange agreements were worked out with banks throughout the country, and BankAmericard went national. Within three years, thirty-five hundred banks and some twenty-six million cardholders were part of its network.

At the same time, a competitive bank cooperative called Interbank merged with a new California system called Mastercharge. This amalgamation, conceived in part because many banks didn't want Bank of America's name on their cards, circulated nearly twenty-two million credit cards. Like BankAmericard, the new group supervised all the interchange and promoted its cards nationally and got a fee of up to twenty-five thousand dollars a year from each of its participating banks plus a small percentage of charge on volume. Each bank billed and collected from its cardholders for their charges.

Cardholders were expected to pay within twenty-five days of billing. If they didn't, an interest charge of 1.5 percent a month would be placed on the outstanding balance. Cash withdrawals on the BankAmericard, which had been added in 1961 and had become the most attractive service offered to members, were extended to a limit of $350 from the original $100. For such use, the interest rate would be the same plus a service charge of 4 percent, so if you borrowed $100 and didn't repay it for a year, you paid $22 in interest on your advance which, of course, was really a bank loan at much higher rates than usual. Interbank charged less for its services. The net profit numbers on bank cards were not overwhelming. There were still no membership fees. Most of the cards were never used, and many of those that were used had been given out indiscriminately.

As witness the great Chicago credit-card fiasco.

"New York isn't fun city," the joke went. "Get a Midwest Bank Card and have the time of your life in Chicago, for free."

In 1966, five Chicago banks, First National, Harris Trust, Central National, Continental Bank, and the Pullman Group, banded together to form their own credit-card operation, the Midwest Bank Card System. Just before Christmas, they mailed out five million unsolicited credit cards to customers and to assorted lists in the Chicago area. It was like a Christmas gift to many who received them and who had neither the wherewithal nor inclination to pay for what they proceeded to charge.

When the dust settled, credit losses from nonpayers was more than 5 percent. In addition, fraud from cards stolen out of mailboxes was at 4 percent. Bank profits declined, and the press had a field day.

The fraud, it turned out, was so high because cards had been sent to people who had been dead for years. Others had been sent to infants and to dogs and cats with peoplelike names who were on lists at pet stores or, in some cases, banks where owners had set up small endowments for them. A dachshund named Alice Griffin got not one but four cards including one that came with a promise that Alice would be welcomed as a "preferred" customer at Chicago's finest restaurants.

Postal workers, handling the credit-card mail glut, in some cases pocketed the cards and went on spending sprees. Sending that many cards out at Christmastime, when temporary workers are employed to help with the normal holiday mail flood, turned out not to have been such a good idea.

Some families who were on welfare or virtually destitute got as many as two dozen cards.

Reaction from the press and from politicians to the bizarre flood of credit cards was swift and contemptuous.

"American banks have mailed 100 million cards to unsuspecting citizens," *Life* magazine reported in 1970, "and have offered each recipient not only a handful of 'instant cash' but a dreamy method of buying by signature after the lettuce runs out."

Wright Patman, chairman of the House Bank Committee, and Senator William Proxmire became longtime critics of the banks. "I think," said Patman, "that the banks, ever since the moneychangers were driven out of the temple of God, have been trying to perfect some plan whereby they can collect from both sides. Credit cards have finally made that possible."

Proxmire was equally disdainful. "Unless we bring unsolicited credit cards under control," he said, "we are likely to produce a nation of credit drunks."

Bank executives shrugged. "It's the name of the game," explained John Sturges, vice-president of retail banking for Continental Bank. "You've got to have a large and active cardholder list." They apparently succeeded on both counts. A year later, the Chicago banks claimed that the cards had generated $100 million in credit-card charges.

It took them several years to sort out the mistakes.

Not included in these charge figures, of course, were thousands of people who shouldn't have gotten credit cards simply because they couldn't afford to buy what they bought with this magic card. They, unlike those who disappeared or simply wouldn't pay, painstakingly repaid bills they should never have run up, getting punished with hefty interest rates in the process.

It was an overt act of greed and carelessness on the part of the banks. From the first, MacNamara's game plan involved careful credit checks so that people who could afford to have the card could have it and those who didn't have the income to support the potential spending the card offered, couldn't. The credit check theoretically worked two ways, protecting the issuer and the potential recipient. The outsized interest rate, of course, eventually changed that for the issuer who could take more chances and lower the barriers. But these were the very marginal credit risks who could and would be hurt.

The banks wanted cardholders even if a few dogs and babies and pet salamanders got cards in the process. They knew that in the long run they'd be okay, even if there were thousands of people who wouldn't be.

A few years later, in its magazine, *Family Banker*, the Continental Bank pontificated to cardholders: "As a smart money manager, there's nothing at all wrong with using credit as an aid to managing your money—it's an accepted way of life. But you must be a manager in actual fact and not let your debts manage you instead."

Voltaire once said, "If a banker jumps out of a window, follow him. On the way down, he'll figure out how to make a profit."

A Federal Reserve study of bank cards in 1968, ignoring the Chicago debacle and relatively similar scenes being played out all over the country, was sanguine about the possibility that credit cards might make their users overborrow. It cited credit limits as one barrier to disaster. It neglected, among other things, to address the growing phenomenon of individuals and families getting any number of cards, unsolicited and otherwise.

The study did state, "Even if cardholders do not overborrow, there is still the danger they will overspend. As credit cards substitute for other means of payments, the traditional signals warning the spender that he is approaching the budget limit are no longer operable—that is, depletion of money from his pocket or exhaustion of the balance in his checkbook no longer sounds an alarm."

The bankers felt good about the way things were going. In 1969, Karl Hinke, chairman of Interbank Card Association—the cooperative credit-card network that was dividing up the bank credit-card world with Bank-Americard—told the American Bankers Association: "We could call the establishment of the bank credit card a new medium of exchange, a renaissance of banking. The credit card of the future will be a membership card in a nationwide electronic-payment and bookkeeping network. It has the potential of eliminating many conventional uses of checks and money."

What they saw was a longtime dream of a "less-check" society coming closer. And it was coming faster than anyone had anticipated. "We're at least two years ahead of schedule," crowed BankAmericard President Donald R. McBride as the seventh decade arrived.

The bank cards were now being accepted by podiatrists, by optometrists for the purchase of eyeglasses, and other stores for such items as hardware and jeans. It was spreading out. American bank cardholders were now charging at the rate of ten billion dollars a year.

In 1970, under the prodding of Patman and Proxmire, Congress passed a law forbidding the mailing of unsolicited credit cards.

It didn't slow things down.

The same year, Gimbel Brothers agreed to test the bank credit-card system by allowing Mastercharge to be honored at its new store in Bridgeport, Connecticut.

The bankers knew they had something—something big. They just didn't know exactly what to do with it. Many of the smaller banks were still losing money on their credit-card operations, but everyone knew it was only a matter of time before the profits from interest rates ranging from 18 percent to 20 percent would heal any of the early wounds. After the initial rush to get large numbers of members, banks started to be more cautious, even doing credit checks on some applicants. However, they never completely discarded the system of offering "pre-approved" credit to those on lists purported to contain people who, at least, hadn't robbed a grocery store or swindled a widow lately.

Jeff Kutler, the senior editor of *American Banker*, the daily newspaper that services the banking industry, says that in the sixties a group of bankers approached the Federal Reserve and asked that institution, which regulates and clears most of the financial paper in the nation, to act as the clearinghouse for credit-card charges. The Fed said no. Kutler feels that had they agreed to do it, we would have lost out on the competition between Visa and MasterCard; that it would have made for "a different dynamic. Card associates would have focused less on technology and even more on selling the card."

In 1969, Mastercharge became the new name for Interbank, and in 1970, Dee Ward Hock, then a forty-one-year-old bank vice-president, would become the head of the BankAmericard operation. In 1977, it became independent of Bank of America, operating on behalf of all of its member banks. BankAmericard, a name that had always stuck in the craw of the other banks participating in the plan, was now changed to Visa. Under Hock's supervision, it would see a card that would be honored extensively at department stores and supermarket chains.

In 1973, Mastercharge developed a central hub to electronically connect the member establishment with the card issuer. This meant that a store owner needing approval on a charge didn't have to phone but just ran the plastic credit card with its new magnetic strip through an electronic machine that had been supplied to him.

The future was here, and it was credit cards.

The banks were as reluctant to charge a fee for the card as MacNamara and Schneider had been in 1950. But in January 1973, the Marquette Bank of Minneapolis imposed an annual membership charge in an attempt to weed out nonusers of the card. It worked. Marquette confirmed what we found at the outset of credit cards. Those who used the cards paid the fee and those who didn't, did not. Within a year, banks all over the country had put in membership dues.

In 1977, laws permitting banks to do business in states other than their own were passed. Citibank, now a vigorous member of the newly renamed Visa plan, dumped twenty-seven million pieces of mail into American homes and offices. Within a few years, it became the biggest issuer of bank credit cards in the world. The twenty-seven-million mailing pieces dwarfed the eight million solicitations sent out to introduce the American Express in 1958 and made the initial mailings I had done in 1951, accompanied by much rolling of the eyes from both MacNamara and Schneider, seem more like a whimper than a roar.

The seventies saw the credit card become the most significant new force in the banking industry. Mastercharge became MasterCard in 1979. It would sit a distant second place to Visa in the eighth decade of the twentieth century, not making a substantial move until the nineties with major company co-branding and new technology.

Although both plans are basically bank cooperatives and are alike in nearly every way, there is a difference. MasterCard is a nonprofit corporation owned by the banks. Visa, owned more or less by the same people, is a we-work-for-profit company. Because they were under a mandate to make money, Visa, particularly in its early years, was more aggressive, more challenging and tougher. By the end of the seventies, it paid off not only with profits, but it made them first, by far.

John Bennett, the former Amex executive who now heads Visa's marketing, crowed about the Visa ad campaign that emphasized Visa's superior service as compared to American Express. MasterCard was never mentioned in the ads, but they implied that there were only two credit cards worth talking about, and MasterCard wasn't one of them.

"We created a two-horse race between Visa and Amex," he told colleagues, "and left MasterCard in the dust."

The seventies also saw the introduction of the debit card, originally called MasterCard II and Electronic Card by Visa. It was a rather elementary system. You deposited money in a bank, and you charged against your balance.

MasterCard, at first, issued debit cards that were identical to their regular credit cards. Visa's were slightly different. Each charged member establishments the same discount for both cards. This created a problem. Why, reasoned the merchant, should we pay you as much for honoring a card on which you have no credit risk. Eventually, both Visa and MasterCard lowered their discount rate on debit cards.

The Diners Club continued to falter under the stewardship of various Continental-appointed executives and was the only one of the major cards to have declining membership in the seventies.

In 1981, Citicorp, with a cautious eye on a possible government antitrust action against Visa and Master-Card's lock on bank credit cards, bought the Diners Club from Continental. It has been estimated that Continental, which had engineered the Diners Club plummet, lost more than $100 million on credit-card operations in the years that it ran the company. Continental has claimed that figure is an exaggeration.

Carte Blanche, never a factor in the credit-card wars, had also been purchased by Citicorp from Avco a year or so before the Diners Club buyout. Like Continental, Avco had lost a considerable amount of money on its credit-card adventure after buying the company from

Hilton in the midsixties. Now, Citicorp owned two independent credit-card companies, and if the Feds decided to break up the Visa-MasterCard monopolies, Citicorp could, if necessary, siphon membership into the Diners Club and Carte Blanche systems.

In the Reagan years, of course, antitrust meant only that you couldn't trust a liberal, and no investigations or suits were forthcoming. Diners Club would emphasize corporate memberships and regain not only posture of sorts but profits that were not as meaningful as their major competitors, but, hey, they weren't losses.

American Express, on the other hand, would prosper in the seventies and eighties despite enormous corporate problems including the infamous salad-oil scandal in which huge tanks of salad oil that had been carried on American Express' inventory books turned up as never having existed. It cost the company sixty million dollars.

In 1977, Howard Clark, who had led the credit-card plan through its losing years and had witnessed its enormous growth, retired. He was replaced as chairman and chief executive officer by James D. Robinson III who guided the company through some uneasy years, particularly when after a typically 1980s period of gestating other companies, he was forced to get rid of many of them.

Married to a public relation's powerhouse, Robinson was more successful at appearing in the gossip columns and on the society-party circuit than as a majordomo and negotiator. An aborted takeover of McGraw-Hill was treated with disdain on the business pages, and a deal he made with Warner's Steve Ross started out as a partnership between the two companies and ended with American Express bailing out for peanuts and Warner's ultimately making huge profits.

American Express' credit-card business would soar primarily because travel by U.S. citizens reached unparalleled heights. Amex's travel agency business also increased and, although never a major moneymaker, was at the core of the traveler's cheque and credit-card business.

Even more satisfying was the growth in traveler's cheque sales. Many had predicted that their sales would diminish with the advent of the credit card; this had been an important reason for Ralph Reed's willingness, after many changes of mind, to go into the credit-card business. But, by the end of the seventies, it appeared that the two could coexist.

It wasn't until the 1990s that sales of traveler's cheques flattened out. Nineteen ninety-four actually showed a slight drop in cheque sales as compared to 1989 despite increases in population and travel. The growth is obviously gone, and it would appear that Reed's worst fears will come to be; the cheque, like bank checks and cash, will go.

In the 1970s, the fee for an American Express card was raised to twenty dollars. It would nearly triple in coming years. Membership would climb steadily until the late 1980s when the bank cards, with their huge marketing edge at the bank level and their offer of buy-now pay-later and their lower charges to member establishments, simply overwhelmed the field.

I had my own credit-card experience after I left the Diners Club in 1967. I'd gathered a group of investors, and we'd put a substantial amount of money in bank accounts as we prepared to enter the magazine-publishing business.

Of course, I already carried a Diners Club card, and when I left the company, American Express sent me a complimentary card as a nod to my involvement in the creation of the first credit card. One day, as a whim, I applied for a Carte Blanche card as well. Two weeks later, I was rejected. I had gone from having Diners Club card number 2 (1002) to being turned down. I later learned that it was a reflection on the newness of my company.

But I had gone the cycle. I had come from being there for the very first credit card to being turned down for one by the company which had let the nineteen-year-old Joseph Miraglia go on his famous spending spree.

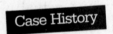 **NUMBER FOUR**
JIMMY AND BELLE—THE SHOPPERS

My good friends who we shall call *Jimmy and *Belle have been married for almost ten years. He's nudging sixty, and she's about fifteen years younger. Let's say Jimmy's an actor (he isn't) and that he makes a lot of money (he does). Over the past thirty years, Jimmy has probably earned between two and three hundred thousand dollars a year as an actor. Some years he earned a lot more. Back in the sixties and seventies, he invested wisely, mostly in California and Colorado real estate which appreciated enormously over the years.

Belle had inherited a restaurant in Santa Monica from her mother when she'd died. It did well, but Belle didn't like the restaurant business. She'd show up at the end of the evening, empty the cash register, and leave. Unfortunately, she neglected to leave enough money to pay the bills, and within a year, the place closed.

When Belle and Jimmy met, it was love at first sight, and they were married soon after. On their honeymoon, Belle told Jimmy she had no credit cards. Well, he had six, so he added her name to his accounts, and soon she, too, had six.

He discovered she had interesting buying habits. And that she'd had no credit cards because the stores and card companies had closed all her accounts for nonpayment. She'd spend hours and hours in malls and department stores. If she saw something she liked, let's say a skirt, she'd buy it in every color it came in. If she liked the look of a pair of shoes, she'd buy five pairs of the same shoes. "She's a riot," Jimmy would tell friends. "Shopping is her way of life."

Well, he had plenty of money and income from real estate, and he was working regularly. Little by little, he started sharing her enthusiasm for shopping. He'd buy the same hundred-dollar shirt in six colors and gadgets—he loved gadgets. He built a miniature sound stage in his own basement which he certainly didn't need or use. They had six rooms in their house and seven television sets. They had recorders and exercise machines that they never used and machines that massaged you and soothed you and sang to you over the sound of surf. Soon, he was buying as many things as she was.

His agent wasn't coming up with as much work for him, but they kept on spending. They traveled constantly and they entertained royally. A hundred guests would cram into their house for a barbecue, and waiters and bartenders would dole out food and drinks in huge quantities.

Cash got tighter, and Jimmy sold off properties to pay bills.

They now had twenty-three credit cards with a total line of credit of more than a quarter of a million dollars.

And they didn't stop spending.

At one point they owned four cars.

Then a baby was born, a strapping boy. Well, they needed a full-time nanny and part-time baby sitters and everything else that goes with having a kid if you're rich.

But they didn't seem to notice that they really weren't rich anymore.

He sold off the last of his properties. She bought six of the most darling little sailor suits at Nordstrom's department store at eighty-nine bucks a suit. "He goes through them so quickly," she explained.

His agent never called. Jimmy simply wasn't working, and the kid was in nursery school at ten thousand a year. They still traveled, mostly with the kid and the nanny, and they still had parties for one hundred.

Jimmy charged a computer for five thousand dollars to keep his acting jobs and finances straight, but he had no jobs and no income—and they didn't know how to use a computer. The nanny didn't know either. So it just sat there, unused, with the exercise machines and the machines that massage the back of your neck.

He decided that they had better start exhibiting some fiscal responsibility. He canceled all of their credit cards but one. Within a month they had gone over the credit limit on the one card. So, they reapplied and got two more.

They are now about $160,000 in debt, a turnaround in net worth of, perhaps, $2 million. He's working again but only occasionally. When he does work, he makes good money, but he's pulling down a lot less than he did in the good "old" days. They're down to three cars and still have the same nanny. They don't throw the big parties anymore. Something's got to go when austerity kicks in.

"You know," he told me recently, "I think Belle's got this shopping thing beat."

"I think," Belle told my wife soon after, "that Jimmy's in control of his credit-card spending now."

We don't really believe either one of them.

Chapter Twelve

CLIPPINGS

NEW YORK TIMES, May 28, 1994: The House of Representatives has approved tax legislation that would authorize the Internal Revenue Service to collect income tax payments by credit card in addition to the checks and money orders now accepted. The legislation allows the IRS to begin negotiations with credit-card issuers. Senate approval is also required.

Beyond the obvious advantage to taxpayers of being able to prolong paying their taxes for as long as they're willing to continue paying high-interest rates on their outstanding debt, the *Times* pointed out the interesting possibilities regarding the advantages to the cardholder of earning enormous amounts of frequent flyer mileage on substantial tax payments. For example, a person paying fifty thousand dollars in taxes with an airline-sponsored credit card could probably get a free trip to Europe each year.

The *Times* suggested that since the cardholder, the card issuer, and the government all seem to think this is a good idea, the Senate would almost certainly pass the bill as well.

WALL STREET JOURNAL, January 12, 1994: Mellon Bank Corporation of Pittsburgh is now offering a credit card that promises to refund all the interest you have paid over a twenty-year period. Such a rebate would amount to $8,667 for the average MasterCard holder whose monthly credit card balance is $2,421. All you have to do is use the card once a year, and the interest will be prorated.

ASSOCIATED PRESS, Business News, April 1, 1993: The J. C. Penney Company now honors the Discover Card for charges at its store and mail-order catalog. The principal owner of Discover is Sears, who, since the nineteenth century, has been Penney's fiercest competitor.

U. S. NEWS & WORLD REPORT, April 9, 1990: The latest recommendation from Japan, proposed in recent trade talks between the two countries, is that Americans should curtail excessive consumer spending by limiting themselves to two credit cards each. Surveys they had authorized revealed that the average U.S. consumer carried between six and seven credit cards (retail, all-purpose, gas, etc.) and that credit-card debt had risen from $53 billion in 1979 to $214 billion ten years later.

THE GLOBE, June 22, 1993: Wallets stuffed with credit cards are creating a condition called "credit-carditis." It gives people who sit on fat wallets a pain in the butt by pressing on the sciatic nerve.

U.S.A. TODAY, September 25, 1991: Citicorp, the number-one issuer of credit cards, is testing the first stages of a computer that can authenticate signatures and will help ease credit-card fraud.

At first, the electronic system will store only signatures, but even that will help resolve disputes and errors as well as control forgery. Instead of a paper sales-draft, credit-card users will sign a form that appears right on a display screen. The screen automatically translates the signature into digital form that can be stored and retrieved electronically. Experts say all retailers will be using such devices by the beginning of the twenty-first century.

LOS ANGELES TIMES, September 24, 1994: Maryland-based Chevy Chase Savings Bank has now introduced Rolling Stones' MasterCard and Visa cards bearing the band's lips-and-tongue logo. "We're delighted to be affiliated with those legendary performances," said Visa Vice-president Barbara Huasta. Users get discounts at participating music stores and earn points good for discounts on Rolling Stones catalog merchandise.

"The thirty-year-old bank actually predates modern credit cards by a few years," stated either the bank or the *Times. Wrong!* Any way you look at it, what with the Diners Club being forty-four years old and the bank card, a creaky thirty-five.

THE GLOBE, December 3, 1991: A new musical credit card will prevent you from forgetting to put your card away after you use it. The card, produced by Majima Company of Japan, plays a song when it's exposed to light after you open your wallet and keeps playing until you restore it to a dark area.

THE NILSON REPORT, October, 1992: Telemarketing has become the credit-card industry's most important marketing medium. In 1992, third-party telemarketers, hired by the credit-card companies, will make 235 million calls to potential customers. In-house telemarketing, primarily bank credit-card systems, will make another 55 million pitches. It is estimated that in 1994, the number will total more than 400 million calls for the year.

GLAMOUR magazine, September, 1991: "Although credit-card issuers routinely deny it, we've heard from several people that many issuers seem to have a policy of waiving the annual fee for 'good' customers (those who have paid their bills on time and charge a certain amount and paid a certain amount in interest during the previous year). The catch is that you may have to ask for this courtesy. We tried it and it worked."

WEEKLY WORLD NEWS, October 13, 1992: Folks with lousy credit ratings are finding a new way out of their financial troubles. For anywhere from thirty-nine to fifteen hundred dollars, consumers across the country are signing up with fly-by-night agencies that promise to polish up their credit images after bankruptcies or financial disaster. They receive a variety of services, ranging from booklets telling them how to have their credit report changed to how to get a complete new identity with fake social-security cards, new drivers' licenses, and other ID.

THE NILSON REPORT, May, 1994: Fingerprint images that can be captured and fed into computers as a low-cost cardholder-identification system are being tested as part of an agreement between Identicator Corporation and the American Bankers Association. Among those already using the process are criminal justice systems and government welfare programs. The manufacturer says it's a surefire way to prevent credit cards from being used by the wrong people.

TIME magazine, May 9, 1994: At the Chemical Bank in New York, automated teller machines mistakenly deducted a total of sixteen million dollars from 100,000 customer accounts in February because of a typographical error in a single line of computer code. The bank bounced thousands of checks as a result.

WALL STREET JOURNAL, December 11, 1991: TRW, the giant credit-reporting system, has settled lawsuits with nineteen states and the Federal Trade Commission and has agreed to sweeping new procedures to make its credit-reporting business fairer to consumers. TRW has conceded that it routinely fills its credit reports with errors and has ignored consumer efforts to correct them.

THE ULTIMATE CREDIT HANDBOOK by Gerri Deteiler, published 1993: One study showed that 40 percent of all credit reports contain erroneous information—some of it quite serious.

LOS ANGELES TIMES, August 14, 1994: The Federal Trade Commission will soon begin shaping rules requiring for the first time that credit-reporting agencies disclose and interpret all your "credit scores," the little understood but highly influential rankings that frequently determine whether you get a loan or a credit card or not.

A score might reflect how many times you paid late on a credit card, for example, or how many open lines of credit you have or how big a down payment you made on the purchase of your last home.

All this information and more is put into a computer which gives you a score that roams anywhere between zero and one thousand.

Scores change as your credit files change which is why the FTC wants the consumer to have access to them so they can make sure they've been updated.

"The idea," said Ed Mierzwinski, consumer program director for the U.S. Public Interest Research Group, which has urged the disclosures, "is for people to get as full and as relevant a disclosure as possible about what creditors are obtaining on them."

PRESS RELEASE, the office of the governor, Maryland, May 14, 1993: The State of Maryland today announced that it has officially implemented the nation's first "debit card" for welfare recipients. Governor Donald Schaefer said today that, "The Independence Card will allow welfare families to 'charge' for food and other related needs to a preset deposit given to them by the state, much like an ATM card. The card will replace food stamps and checks normally granted for welfare family support."

It is anticipated that this new policy will sharply decrease food-stamp theft and misuse and theft of welfare checks, a perennial problem among welfare recipients. The state also expects to save millions of dollars annually in handling and documentation costs.

MIAMI HERALD, June 6, 1994: Citibank, which issues both Visa and MasterCard credit cards and now vigorously promotes its new photo ID card, says fraud losses have been cut by about two-thirds since it began issuing the free card.

BROCHURE issued by the New York City Transit Commission, January 6, 1994: Beginning March 15, you'll be able to purchase a MetroCard, a thin plastic card that will, by 1997, replace coins and tokens on all of New York's subways and buses and on the Long Island Rail Road. Actually, a debit card, you purchase MetroCards for any amount up to eighty dollars, and each fare is deducted as you use the card. A magnetic strip on your card records your charges. Readers installed at transit authority stations will enable you to check your balance at all times.

SAN FRANCISCO CHRONICLE, December 26, 1991: The number of personal bankruptcy filings jumped by 24 percent in the twelve months ended September 30, increasing in every region of the country.

SAN FRANCISCO CHRONICLE, February 16, 1989: A San Francisco jury has returned a $5.2 million verdict against Wells Fargo Bank, finding that the fees were too

harsh for customers who paid their bills late or over-
spent their credit-card limits.

"Wells Fargo violated the law," said James C.
Sturdevant, one of the consumer attorneys.

Weyman L. Lundquist, attorney for the bank, said
bank officials felt victorious because the consumer
attorneys had first claimed damages of thirty million
dollars, then offered to settle the case for fifteen million
dollars.

"Wells Fargo believes that those who cause the costs
should have to pay the costs," he stated.

"The bank's Visa and MasterCard customers must
pay their bills within a month [twenty-five days]," the
article said, and the bank charges three to five dollars
when those payments are late. Customers who exceed
their credit limits by 15 percent or more are subject to
a ten dollars monthly fee.

The consumer attorneys pegged the monthly administrative costs of late payments at a maximum of $1.89
and no more than $1.08 for over-the-limit payments and
argued that the finance (interest) charge of 20 percent
already covered the banks costs.

WALL STREET JOURNAL, March 16, 1992: The California
Supreme Court refused to review a lower court's find-
ings that Wells Fargo Bank imposed $5.2 million in ille-
gal fees on more than a million credit cardholders.

NEW YORK TIMES, September 6, 1994: Mondex, a "smart
card" being developed in England, is one of the credit
cards that carries a computer chip and can be loaded

with "money" at an ATM or through a special telephone, then used to buy items of any price merely by transferring funds from the card to an inexpensive terminal which people can have in their homes or stores or offices. According to Mondex Senior Executive Michael Keegan, it provides the anonymity vital to acceptance.

"If you want to have a product that replaces cash, you have to do everything cash does, only better," says Keegan. "With the Mondex Smart Card, you can give money to your brother who gives it to the chap that sells newspapers, who gives it to charity, who puts it in the bank, which has no idea where it's been. That's what money is."

A trial run of Mondex is scheduled for Swindon, England, in 1995.

RICHMOND TIMES-DISPATCH, Richmond, Virginia, September 22, 1993: Credit-card collecting may be the next hot hobby. This Saturday hundreds of credit card and phone collectors from all over the world will meet in Richmond to buy, sell, and trade cards. "One thing you have to have to be successful at this hobby," says organizer Jerry Ballard, "is a good credit rating." Greg Tunks, publisher of *The Credit Card Collector*, a monthly newsletter, complains, "The credit-card industry doesn't recognize the historical significance of the cards. They don't save specimens of the cards they issue.

"Baseball-card manufacturers endorse collecting and marketing collectors' items. Credit-card companies don't support or encourage collections."

FROM A REPORT to members of The American Credit Collector's Association by credit-card collector Jerry Ballard, August 25, 1994: "Credit cards are currently valued at up to $1,500 each. I know a person who'll pay $1,500 for a 1950 Diners Club card in any condition. A used paper 1958 American Express Card sold recently for $530. Two years ago, a 1958 Diners Club booklet card sold for $350."

LIN OVERHOLT'S CARD TRADER NEWSLETTER, August, 1994: At a Las Vegas auction conducted by auctioneers Butterfield and Butterfield over this past June 18 weekend, an American Express credit card which once belonged to Elvis Presley was purchased for $41,400. The buyer was TV star John Corbett who plays the starry-eyed disc jockey on *Northern Exposure*. The card expired in May of 1974.

PRESS RELEASE, U.S. Postal Service, June 22, 1993: The U.S. Postal Service announced today it has begun accepting credit and ATM cards at 555 post offices in the Dallas-Fort Worth, Orlando, and Washington, D.C. areas.

Post offices in other cities will phase in the program beginning in the spring of 1994. Credit cards will be accepted at all post offices by 1995.

LOS ANGELES TIMES, March 26, 1994: The Florida Marlins baseball team now is accepting credit cards for hot dogs, soda, and peanuts at their ball park.

THE NILSON REPORT, May, 1994: The amount U.S. credit-card issuers charged off to fraud (theft, counterfeiting, criminal use of lost cards, etc.) for 1993 totaled $1.78 billion. This, despite new techniques in holograms used in printing cards, photo-identification, and cardholder and card authentication now built right into the card's magnetic strip. It is anticipated that fraud, which costs the credit-card companies 14.2 cents on every 100 dollars spent, will be responsible for more than 14 billion dollars in credit-card losses between 1994 and the year 2000.

NEW YORK TIMES, March 12, 1994: The most profitable department of full-service commercial banks in the U.S. is now their credit-card service. They're so profitable that banks are spinning off their credit-card units into publicly held companies for capital gains as well as increases in the net worth of their existing stock since they retain the majority of the stock in the new company which immediately has a high market value.

THE NILSON REPORT, June, 1994: VeriFone, the company producing sixty percent of the computer terminals used by merchants to verify credit-card charges, has now introduced the "folio" portable terminal which enables restaurant patrons to pay at their table without handing their card to their waiter. Diners verify the amount entered by the waiter, indicate whether payment is to be credit or debit, swipe their card through the readers, enter the PIN, and, if desired, add a tip. The data is transferred electronically to the establishment terminal for authorization. Nilson suggests it could become popular with casinos for gamblers who want to buy chips on their credit card without leaving the gambling table.

A GALLUP POLL, 1961: A survey called "Careless Americans —a report on how people lose cash" found that nearly ten million adults had lost (not stolen or mislaid) cash totaling more than $700 million in the first nine months of 1961. The typical answer as to how the money was lost: "Don't know. First it was there, and then it wasn't."

FROM AN INTERVIEW with Eugene Lockhart, president and CEO, MasterCard: "The day I got this job, I got home around eight o'clock at night. As I walked through the door, there was a phone call for me from a telemarketing firm representing a MasterCard bank. He didn't know anything about my situation, but he wanted to know if I was interested in charging for a new form of unemployment insurance they were selling."

CBS-TV EVENING NEWS, September 30, 1994: "Twenty-eight percent of all U.S. credit-card fraud is perpetrated in the state of California."

CREDIT CARD MANAGEMENT magazine, February, 1993: MasterCard scored a coup last December when the New Jersey division of Law and Public Safety and the California Department of Motor Vehicles became the first state agencies in the country to pay the card-issuer's discount fee without passing the charge on to the cardholder. Until then, people charging their speeding tickets or motor vehicle registrations also paid the card company's discount.

FORTUNE magazine, October, 1988: Jerry Falwell's *Old Time Gospel Hour* and Robert Schuler's *Hour of Power* have long accepted credit cards as has the Church of Scientology. At Jimmy Swaggart's ministries in Baton Rouge, a staffer cheerfully answers the phone with "Visa and MasterCard accepted."

NATIONAL EXAMINER, October 12, 1993: Kevin Kusek, an employee of a body-removal service, searched the clothing of corpses he picked up, retrieving such information as social-security numbers, addresses, and employment. He'd then apply for credit cards under the names of the deceased, giving his own address. A credit-card clearinghouse clerk noticed that a lot of applications were coming in with the same "new" address. Kusek was arrested and had to pay back the nearly five thousand dollars that he'd already taken in cash advances.

THE GLOBE, July 23, 1992: Veteran character actor Robert Morley, who died this month, had told his family he was sure he'd need his plastic in the next world. Morley, known for such films as *The African Queen* and *Around the World in Eighty Days*, was buried, as requested, with his Amex, Visa, and MasterCard cards.

LOS ANGELES TIMES, October 24, 1993: The hot new trend in money management involves putting your home equity onto a gold Visa or other credit card. You then convert your entertainment, dining, travel, and other personal-expenses-related debt—with all interest fully deductible against your federal and state taxes. You are then paying off your charge-account balances with interest payments, not of fifteen percent or eighteen percent but as low as seven percent.

AMERICAN BANKER magazine, May, 1993: The banking committee of the California state legislature, which last month defeated a plan backed by consumer groups to limit card rates to the interest paid by banks on savings accounts plus ten percent, have now approved a bill which would enable banks in the state to impose higher fees on cardholders who are late in paying.

VISA, PRESS RELEASE, August 3, 1994: Visa International announced today that it has acquired the electronic bank and bill payment operations of Virginia-based U.S. Order and that, through a newly formed subsidiary card Visa Interactive, will enter the market with an advanced, fully operational electronic banking and bill payment system. Ed Jensen, president and CEO of Visa, stated that, "Visa institutions will take banking into the home, office—anywhere their customers are. Consumers will have their own personal bank branch wherever their computer is."

Next year, Visa Interactive will introduce "E Pay," a fully postable electronic billing and bill-payment service which will allow Visa merchants to deliver statements and invoices, cardholders to pay their bills electronically, and financial institutions to settle these transactions by debiting the consumer's bank account and crediting the biller, all via interactive computers.

NEW YORK TIMES, August 12, 1994: Yesterday, Phil Brandenberger bought a compact audio disk, paid for it with his credit card, and made history.

"He made the purchase from his office in Nashua, New Hampshire, where, using a secret code, he sent his

Visa credit card number through his computer to buy the $12.48 disk.

"'Even if the National Security Agency was listening in, they couldn't get his credit card number,' said Daniel M. Kohn, the twenty-one-year-old chief executive of the Net Market Company of Nashua. The order was processed using a powerful data encryption software designed to guarantee privacy.

"Major organizations working on rival systems heralded the achievement. 'Most companies want security and privacy when sending credit-card numbers over computers before committing to significant electronic commerce,' said Cathy Medich, executive director of Commercenet."

For now, the *Times* went on to explain, Mr. Brandenberger will pay his Visa bill with an old-fashioned check and receive his disc via Federal Express.

COMMERCIAL on Arts & Entertainment cable channel, Los Angeles, June 13, 1994: "Penis Enlargement. Painless, sure to add two to four inches. Charge to your Visa, MasterCard, or American Express cards."

Chapter Thirteen

YOU CAN SEE THE TWENTY-FIRST CENTURY FROM HERE AND IT'S A CREDIT-CARD WORLD

"EVENTUALLY," Spencer Nilson told me over dinner recently, "there will be two systems—Visa and Master-Card—only two systems all over the world."

"What about American Express?" I asked.

"The American Express card will exist, but it will have a Visa or MasterCard imprint. They'll be the issuer and the biller, just as Citibank or Bank of America is today, but everything else will be handled by the bank plans."

"And Discover and JCB [Japanese Credit Bureau]?" I asked.

"Same thing," Nilson said emphatically. "A Visa or MasterCard imprint, much like GM or Ford."

The worldwide statistics on credit-and debit-card volume in 1994 seem to indicate that if Nilson isn't right, we are at least heading in that direction at break-neck speed.

In 1993, MasterCard increased its charge volume by 28 percent, Visa by 18 percent. At the same time, American Express charges rose 5 percent, JCB 8 percent, and Diners Club 4 percent.

Total charges on cards issued by worldwide credit-card companies were an astonishing $1,025 trillion.

Of that, Visa volume was $527.49 billion;

MasterCard, $320.62 billion;

Amex, $124.06 billion;

JCB, $32.18 billion;

Diners Club $20.81 billion.

The Discover Card, distributed only in the United States, is not included in the figures.

The worldwide cardholder count at year-end, 1993:

Visa, 331.1 million;

MasterCard, 210.3 million;

American Express, 35.4 million;

JCB, 27.8 million;

Diners Club, 20.81 million.

Bank cards now accounted for 88.6 percent of the number of cards in circulation. They had grown by 49.6 million in 1993 while travel and entertainment cards grew only 1.6 million.

Why this growth has been disproportionate is, of course, not difficult to rationalize.

The bank cards primarily offer time payments. You can borrow money or extend yourself or overextend yourself at your whim. They also offer debit and secured cards for those who can't get credit cards or want to be prudent enough to charge only what they have in the bank.

Bank cards are much easier to get. Because of their interest rates, the banks are willing to take more chances. Because they don't offer time-payments (except for American Express's Optima card plan), the t-and-e cards can't take chances.

In addition, Visa and MasterCard, basically cooperatives, have an enormous number of what amounts to sales offices all over the world in the form of their member banks and their branches. You open an account, you get an application for a credit card. You appear on a mailing list in your community, your local bank sends you an application.

Cardholder numbers, of course, are somewhat misleading since many people have at least several cards issued by different banks and most who have an Amex or Diners Club card also have at least one bank card, but the volume is irrefutable.

By 1950, when the all-purpose card first appeared, all major oil companies issued their own credit cards. For forty-three years, the majority of all credit-card purchases at U.S. gas stations was charged to those cards. In 1993, for the first time, charges on credit cards other than those issued by the oil companies was greater than volume generated by the company cards.

Department-store charges are heading in the same direction. Another industry whose charge opportunities will eventually be absorbed by the bank cards is long-distance telephone service. Sources estimate the potential charges through Visa and MasterCard will be more than sixty billion dollars a year by the turn of the century. Another reason, one might think, for AT&T going into the bank credit-card business. Experts in the communications industry predict that most charge purchases in the twenty-first century will not be made with merchant-issued cards but through the two bank-card systems. "And," they emphasize, "we're not talking only about America. We're talking *world*."

In its barest elements, the Visa and MasterCard systems are simply overall promotional and clearinghouses for member banks. The banks actually solicit, check credit, and issue the cards. When the card is used, MasterCard and Visa computer systems approve the charges and direct them to the bank that issued the card.

The merchant or charge service actually brings or sends receipts of all charges to the member bank he does business with. They pay him, deducting whatever service fee has been agreed on.

Now, the bank that has issued the actual credit card used in the transaction gets the charge information from Visa or MasterCard and bills the member. Each bank is responsible for its own collections and credit losses. A small interchange fee is paid to the "card-issuing" bank by the "merchant" bank.

What, more precisely, do Visa and MasterCard do? They, mostly, vigorously promote the name, set standards and rules but not interest rates or credit policies, handle the aforementioned interchanges of charges through their vast computer networks, control a central authorization center, and operate a far-flung antifraud army. They also often make the big deals—like signing worldwide or nationwide charge services: hotel chains, airlines, and chain stores.

In the 1967 film, *The Graduate*, a wise businessman advises recent college graduate Dustin Hoffman to think "plastics" when contemplating a career. "Computers" would have been even better advice. And computers are what make the bank cards work. Without them, the bank credit-card system would not exist. The Diners Club flourished without computers because it was a wholly owned, tightly run company basically under one (actually two) roofs. The bank credit-card networks are sprawled under tens of thousands of roofs. Only the high-tech computers we know today can keep them running.

At its height in prebank card days, the Diners Club worldwide membership barely exceeded 2,000,000, and, as noted, the two bank associations have more than 541,000,000 cards in circulation. Try handling that with a battery of little old ladies reading and filing charges with the naked eye and by hand.

Frank MacNamara gave a veritable handful of businessmen an opportunity to charge for their lunches at a goodly number of select restaurants, but it has been the computer that ushered in the magic age where anybody can charge almost anywhere for virtually anything.

Make that *anywhere*, the "almost" being unnecessary. For example, MasterCard credits an enormous surge in charge volume in China in 1993 as being one of the principal reasons for its dramatic 28 percent leap for the year. China has now become the world's second-largest market by volume. Nearly all their cards are debit cards.

"We're going to replace checks and cash with charge cards and deposit access [debit cards]," Visa says in a report to stockholders. They go on to emphasize, as does MasterCard, the widening world market.

And both companies continually emphasize the new technology, basically computer technology, that has perfected interchange, the battle against fraud and counterfeiting, and the constant honing of the system to make it more efficient.

Read the bank-card reports and voluminous information booklets, talk to their executives, and you will constantly hear about new electronic systems that are refining the new currency.

In 1988, MasterCard, searching for a competitive edge over Visa, rethought its marketing approach. One decision was to urge its member banks to go all out for the blue-collar user. Stop emphasizing glamour and play up everyday use—and lower your credit standards, the banks were told

Visa, of course, soon followed suit.

The resultant mass distribution of credit cards to people, many of whom didn't need them and couldn't afford to pay for what they bought, took us another giant step closer to a debtor economy. Once again, the banks figured that volume would cure their collection problems and it did. As usual, the banks didn't get hurt— only people did. As usual, the bad debts rose but even those figures were deceptive. It was not only the people would couldn't pay who were injured but the people who could—but barely. There are no statistics of the families that struggle to pay bills they probably should never have incurred but came because credit was made so available, so attractive, so seemingly painless.

MasterCard also took a good, hard look at affinity cards and co-branding. In 1985, both card systems had already made a strong move with relationships with American Airlines (Aadvantage Plan) and other carriers. Cardholders, of course, liked the idea of getting free mileage as a bonus for their credit-card use.

Before 1988, such companies as Merrill Lynch had offered bank cards to members, agreeing to make donations to charities and causes and even political organizations based on member spending. This was the affinity card. North Carolina's Department of Agriculture, for example, sponsors a Visa card that contributes a percentage of purchases to promoting the state's agricultural products.

In 1988, Southern New England Telephone debuted the first co-branded bank card other than the airlines, offering bonus discounts on phone rates to card users. It was the beginning of a marketing campaign which has resulted in a wide assortment of benefits to cardholders and millions of new members to the bank-card companies.

In 1990, AT&T offered a Visa or MasterCard to their customers, and one million people applied for cards in a seventy-eight-day period, an unprecedented sales effort. Soon major companies in diverse industries were offering the cards along with rebates, discounts, and other assorted awards.

In February of 1992, General Motors announced that it would participate in the issuance of co-branded

MasterCard credit cards, giving users rebates on GM cars with no fee for the card.

It was the most resounding marketing coup in credit-card history. One million cards were requested in thirty days, two million in sixty days. GM-MasterCard membership is currently at six million.

As of January 31, 1994, GM cardholders had earned $810 million in rebates on autos. Nearly $40 million had already been redeemed. Discounts were involved (the average discount was $300) in the purchase of nearly 123,000 GM cars.

After the GM onslaught, Visa, which had not been as aggressive in the co-branding business as MasterCard, dove in. Affiliates of both systems are now busily romancing major companies. In each case, the company joins not only with Visa or MasterCard, or both as in the case of American Airlines, but with a particular bank such as American Airlines did with Citibank and AT&T with Universal Bank or Shell Oil with Chemical Bank. In some cases, the affiliation is with banks actually owned by the company involved.

More than nineteen thousand banks or other types of financial institutions around the world form Visa while some twenty-one thousand such institutions are members of MasterCard. Many offer both cards. Member banks add their own flourishes to the card and do battle within the Visa and MasterCard framework and name.

Thus, Citibank, the leading bank issuer in the world, popularized the frequent-flyer plan for which members pay fifty dollars a year dues but has virtually eliminated an annual fee for its regular no-frills, no gimmicks, no-bonuses credit card so it can compete with other bank cards. Chase Manhattan, the third largest domestic issuer of credit cards, has now come up with a cash-rebate plan. The gimmicks created to entice new members and to get old members to charge more descend on us in ever-increasing waves. Some of the executives I spoke to in the course of writing this book weren't themselves sure how everything they were offering to the public worked.

I remember sitting on the terrace of a Florida hotel with Ralph Schneider in the midfifties. The Diners Club, of course, then virtually stood alone in the credit-card world. He was in a somewhat philosophical mood.

"You know what we're selling?" he asked me, not really expecting or wanting an answer. "Bullshit!" he exclaimed after a brief pause. "We have no product. It's a service you really don't need and a convenience we've invented. People did business and traveled and paid their way thousands of years before we came along."

That was forty years ago, and the world had not yet become the tight little globe it is now; a place where accessibility to all parts of one's country and, indeed, to many other countries, is a matter of hours and where computers and fax machines have accelerated both the pace of living and the velocity of doing business. Speed may kill but it also counts, and the quickness and efficiency of one credit card, one bill, one check is indisputable.

With the adding of the prepaid debit card to the credit-card arsenal, the banks have made what once was impossible, possible. The constant flow of new services, new ways you can use your card, edges us closer and closer to the death of cash.

The banks have also overwhelmed the credit-card industry and the credit cardholder. With an endless access to money, with daily contact with consumers, with the sheer weight of the name "banker," they now have their own monetary system, one that they totally dominate. By relying on volume to cure any of their bad-debt problems, they have created a new society of debtors. The government has refused to intercede on behalf of the consumer who pays exorbitant interest rates or the unfortunates who haven't been able to stay away from the free lunch. The banks themselves, despite their participation in the two cooperative card systems, fight one another at the consumer's expense. Competition may have made America great, but in the credit-card wars, bankers fall over each other to get more charge cards to consumers already drawing easy credit.

"Banking," someone once said, "has no conscience, only statistics."

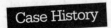 **NUMBER FIVE**
SHERI—THE GIRL FRIEND

New Yorker Sheri Block is another who found that love and credit cards are compatible. The attractive divorcee put an ad in the personals columns in *New York* magazine. She found wealthy advertising executive Jay Levinson. For months they carried on a romance clouded only by his not being able to spend evenings with her. He was a widower, he told her, and had to be home at night with his two motherless children. Then one day she called his home in New Jersey—and the woman who answered identified herself as his wife.

Over Sheri's copious tears, he explained that his first wife had died and that this was his second wife who he was in the process of divorcing. There was still doubt, and after a couple of months, Sheri investigated and discovered that indeed it was his second wife who had answered the phone in New Jersey but that his "dead" first wife was actually still alive and—it was entirely possible that he was still married to her, too.

Again, she tearfully confronted him with the facts she had gathered. This time he didn't deny them but swore that she was the only woman he loved.

To prove it, he gave her an American Express card which he guaranteed. She used it conservatively and all was well, until, a few months later, she discovered that he had still-another girl friend. He now was involved, one way or another, Sheri believed, with two wives and two girl friends, including her.

No more tears! Now she was mad!

In three days she and the American Express card went on a forty-thousand-dollar shopping spree. (He was apparently not only a man of unlimited energy but of unlimited resources.) She bought Armani and Chanel clothing and imported handbags. One outfit alone cost eighteen hundred dollars.

Finally, American Express called Levinson about the excessive use of the card. He immediately reported it stolen. When they finally found Sheri and she told them her story, the Amex representative exclaimed, "Honey, you should have bought more!"

Now, Levinson's suing her for unauthorized credit-card purchases.

She's suing him for harassment because of the nasty phone call he made to her after her spree.

The American Express bill has been settled.

No word from the one or, possibly, two wives.

Chapter Fourteen

MY CARD
IS BETTER THAN
YOUR CARD

THE BATTLE OF the credit card giants makes the Coca-Cola\Pepsi fracas seem like a kindergarten scratch-fest. It makes the General Motors-Ford-Chrysler triumvirate seem like Damon and Pythias. It makes those television comparison tests for rival headache remedies seem like family reunions. American Express and Visa claw at each other in their TV ads like two bobcats in heat. The Discover Card sues Visa. Executives of both MasterCard and Visa drop venom about their nearest rival in speeches and in interviews.

Why don't these people like each other?

Because there's really not a spit's worth of difference between the cards except for numbers.

Other than the varied interest rates and generally overstated rebate programs, one man's Visa is basically another man's Visa. Since all banks in both plans offer the same basic merchant charge services, they are constantly coming up with other reasons one should carry their Visa card and not the Visa card of that bank around the corner.

Nasty little charges for late payments or going beyond one's credit limit will vary, but otherwise it's all pretty much the same. With the advent of co-branding, cardholders, who almost seem indifferent to the fact that some banks charge 18 percent interest per annum and others less than 10 percent, suddenly got more enthused about merchandise and service rebates. This, despite the fact that the rebates they receive almost always involve saving less money than the lower interest rates.

Loretta Mester, an economist for the Federal Reserve, has completed a paper which theorizes that the people most likely to shop for low credit-card interest rates are those with low balances. Cardholders who use the cards a lot seem willing to stay with higher interest rates, mainly because of a reluctance to leave banks where they've already established relationships and higher credit limits.

Ralph Schneider's theory that "We're selling nothing" may not have been true, but no one can deny that, in the credit-card business, the "selling" is the important thing. The co-branding discounts may not add up to a lot of money for the average cardholder but they sound great. "Get a GM credit card and buy a car at a discount."

The experienced car buyer will know, however, that most car dealers will negotiate anyway when it comes to price. Dealers I spoke to say that when they negotiate, they keep all rebates in mind. You don't get it twice.

And, of course, there's a limit on all co-branding credit-card rebates. In the case of GM, the most you can earn each year toward the purchase of a new car is $500. You'd have to charge $10,000 to get that, and you can accumulate your rebates over seven years for a maximum of $3,500.

The interest rate on GM cards is 17 percent or about 7 percent higher than you can pay at various banks for the same Visa or MasterCard. This means that if you carry $10,000 a year on revolving credit, you're paying an extra $700: two hundred bucks more than the rebate. Deduct from that a nominal membership fee frequently charged by the banks offering the lower rates, and you're still losing money on the deal. GM or Ford cardholders who use the card minimally and get equally minimum rebates can get a slight edge, but a rebate of $50 or $100 doesn't seem to be a great enticement when you're buying a $10,000 or $15,000 car.

But it sounds good!

Ford has a slightly higher annual rebate limit, $700, on its co-branded card, but you can only accrue for five years so the maximum total rebate limit is still $3,500.

The offers are so diffuse and change so often that again the customer-relations people don't have simple answers. They frequently have to check with others to give you interest-rate variances and sometimes have to remind you that "this is a new offer and will only last six months."

General Electric, which began by issuing "gift certificates" toward the purchase of products at retailers like K-Mart and Toys 'R' Us, has now switched to cash rebates. They start at 1/2 of 1 percent if you charge up to $2,000 and escalate in steps of $2,000 and 1/2 percentiles with a ceiling of $140 a year. GE has no annual fee and charges interest rates ranging from approximately 15 percent, if you have very good credit, to just under 19 percent, if your credit is at least slightly tarnished or your bank account undernourished.

The AAA co-branding card (MasterCard) charges no fee; gives you a twenty-five day interest-free grace period to pay your bills; tells you the card puts more purchasing power in your pocket; offers checks which you can use to make purchases; allows you to use more than eighty thousand Cirrus ATMs for instant cash; offers free traveler's checks; and tells you that you can charge your AAA dues on your card. Then, Triple A lets you know you can earn member-award points which you can use to save money on your auto-club dues renewal or other club services and products. As in the case of the other rebate plans, the savings are minuscule unless you're a big spender.

All of the above sales points, except the savings on AAA services, are available from almost any bank card in existence, and you pay a variable interest rate of around 15 percent, considerably higher than that offered by numerous issuing banks.

It's hype.

Even the airline discounts are meaningful only to cardholders who spend a lot of money. The American Airlines Aadvantage card, available through both Visa and MasterCard banks and most popular through Citibank, gives you a credit of one frequent-flyer mile for every dollar you charge. But a frequent-flyer mile is not equivalent to an actual air mile. If you live in New

York and want to fly to Los Angeles, a distance of less than three thousand miles, you need twenty thousand frequent-flyer miles. So if you and your wife were fed up with the cold Manhattan winters and wanted to loll on the beach at Laguna, you would have had to have recorded forty thousand dollars in charges to earn two coach-ticket trips. Citibank charges fifty dollars a year for Aadvantage membership (eighty-five dollars for a gold card) and, fiercely competitive, it has dropped its annual interest rates to less than 15.4 percent where it once flirted with the 20 percent mark.

In a move that is unique, Nationsbank of Atlanta offers cardholders a tax-deferred annuity into which the bank puts 1 percent of the cardholder's purchases. Some participating merchants will even add to the package.

It's obvious, however, that if you can steel yourself against the advertising attacks, your best bet would be a card that offers few of the embellishments but has a low interest rate, unless you're someone who charges a lot and flies a lot, then frequent-flyer miles make sense. In this respect, they make so much sense and have been used so often by cardholders with deep pockets and packed luggage that the airlines have started to put limits on the amount of miles you can earn.

But to most people seeking revolving credit, the banks offering comparatively low-interest rates would seem most attractive.

Arkansas Federal Credit Services in Little Rock offers a variable rate of prime plus 1.75 percent. At this writing, prime, as published daily in the *Wall Street Journal*, is 7.25 percent, so they're offering a 9 percent rate. Compare this to Great Western Bank, one of the major California banking institutions with branches in Florida and other states. It still charges around 20 percent on its credit cards and offers straight, unsecured loans, totally independent of its credit-card operation, at 17.5 percent, apparently the norm for larger banks.

So, you can pay more than 10 percent less on credit-card charges through certain banks (usually smaller banks but, what-the-hell, you owe *them* money so who cares how big they are?) and more than 7 percent less than you'd pay on an unsecured loan.

The Wachovia Bankcard of Wilmington, Delaware, has a current rate on its credit-card outstandings of 11.15 percent. Wachovia charges an eighteen-dollar annual fee while Arkansas Federal charges thirty-five dollars but, unlike most banks, puts that 9-percent-interest charge in on day one, not day twenty-six, of your bill.

The Choice Bank in Sioux Falls, South Dakota, has the same rate as Wachovia with a twenty-dollar annual fee, and the Oak Brook Bank, of Oak Brook, Illinois, has an 11.90 percent rate with no annual fee.

Banks will, of course, change rates, but you can always change banks. Some banks, including Great Western, give you a lower rate as a six-month or one-year introductory lure. This most interesting "low introductory" offer came from Bank One a few years ago: they offered a 5.9 rate, at that time actually below the prime rate. In fine print on an enclosed card, however, it was dutifully noted that in a few months hence that rate would increase by approximately ten percentage points to 15.9 percent.

The Signet Bank of Richmond, Virginia, offers you 8.9 percent for the first year. After that it's around 13.9 percent, and they offer you the latest credit card wrinkle; you can charge your balance from other credit cards to your Signet Visa. At 8.9 percent, that's not a bad deal. Signet, however, is notoriously cautious about its credit limits, and big spenders will likely be disappointed.

Wachovia and numerous other banks are offering the same service with slightly higher interest rates, and the Chase Manhattan Bank now tells you to "stop paying the high interest rates charged by incentive cards that give you cash back or free airline tickets and use the Chase Reward Consolidator. It's not a credit card. It's a unique line of credit that enables you to earn credit-card rewards without paying high interest rates on your outstanding balances. You use your reward cards, as usual, earning the rewards as you use the card. Then you simply write a check each month to transfer your balances to your Chase Reward Consolidation line of credit."

Chase's Consolidator variable rate (at this writing) is 11.44 percent. And, there's no annual fee.

Wow! What a great idea! You still get all those free miles, gifts, cash, and you're paying at least a third less interest.

One problem in the offing: the credit-card companies, primarily the co-branding cards and their banks, won't stand for it. They make their money on people who take a long time to pay their bills and pay 15 percent, 16 percent, and more, while they're taking their time. Sure, co-branding is also a sales gimmick to sell cars or extra seats on airlines, but the payoff for the banks is in the high-interest rates.

Something will be done about this. Bet on it. If they're not killing the goose, they're surely beating the hell out of it. James Daley, editor of *Credit Card News*, a trade publication, described the plan thusly: "It is one of the most novel pirating schemes that I've ever heard of."

About 28 percent of all bank cardholders pay their bills within the twenty-five day, no interest, limit. They, of course, are getting the rebates without paying the freight, but 72 percent apparently can't afford to do that or don't chose to.

The cunning credit cardholder will use his Aadvantage card to run up his bills, then pay his credit-card bill with a Wachovia or Chase lower-interest, pay-your-bills-plan.

As we've said, despite the disparities, the interest rate doesn't, so far, seem to be the user's principal reason for selecting a credit card. Citibank, GM, Ford, AT&T, Chase Manhattan, and other major issuing banks and co-branding companies are charging significantly higher interest rates than many smaller bank card issuers but still dominate the market.

Citibank's decision to drop the membership fee for their regular and gold cards (not Citibank Aadvantage) will cost them an estimated $150 million in 1994, and, as covered earlier, they have also lowered their interest rates. They'll get some of it back by assessing revolving-credit customers a payment of 1/36th of their balance, up from 1/48th. Customers who fail to make minimum payments within fifteen days of the due date will be assessed fees of fifteen dollars every fifteen days, about double what they were charged before. These two adjustments will net Citibank about $60 million of the $150 million they'll lose on the waiver of fees.

The credit-card field has become fiercely competitive, and one can understand the constant drive to add sales ploys to get people to charge more and more *for* more. Whether they can afford or need more has never been the issue. "It doesn't matter," one industry leader said in answer to this thought. "People *always* bought things they couldn't afford or didn't need."

Agreed, to an extent. Bank credit cards, however, have certainly enabled them to go further up that path and to make the trip more often and more easily. "It's convenient" was one of the pitches we used to sell Diners Club cards with. But the very convenience could be a serious problem to people living on the edge.

Offering that convenience, however, is a winner.

A meticulous study in the August 1991 issue of Harper's magazine by Glen von Nostitz and Michael Alcamo revealed that profits from the then-thirty-one million Citibank Visas and MasterCards outstanding in 1990 were almost one billion dollars—half of which went to offset losses in other Citicorp divisions. "Burdened with some thirteen billion dollars in non-performing loans," the article stated, "Citicorp officials believe that legions of mall-goers, shouldering Citibank credit cards, will lead the company back into the black by edging themselves into the red."

The borrowed "Reagan prosperity," the S and L debacles, and the general mismanagement of large corporations by acquisition-happy know-nothings financed by pie-in-the-sky Wall Street gamblers body-slammed the economy and sent the banks reeling. The *Harper's* article reflected, "Citicorp's delinquent real estate loans constitute 29 percent of its total real estate portfolio. The average commercial real estate delinquency rate for the nation's fifteen money-center banks is 20 percent. Clearly, holders of credit cards are being forced to cough up money lost by others."

Real-estate loan problems have abated, and the enormous losses banks suffered from foreign loans have, more or less, been controlled, but the lesson was painfully learned. Better to loan a billion dollars to a million people at 18 percent than a billion to one uneasy company or country at prime.

Citibank credit-card volume in 1993 rose to $55 billion, more than the next two U.S. bank card issuers (First Chicago and AT&T Universal) combined. England's Barclay Bank is actually closer to Citibank in credit-card volume than either, with $35.16 billion in 1993. The Bank of China was third with nearly 25 billion in charges. Chase Manhattan, once second in the credit-card race, tumbled to eleventh place primarily because of the impact co-branding with GM, GE, and AT&T had in the market and because foreign banks are now a force in credit-card matters. Bank of America, the first major bank to enter the credit-card field and the company which gave birth to Visa, is now the twelfth largest issuer, still high considering their interest rate to credit cardholders remains at a fraction under 20 percent.

In fifth place with volume of more than $17 billion is MBNA America, an issuer of Visa and MasterCard credit cards to special-interest groups, founded and headed by an astute entrepreneur by the name of Charles Cawley. While companies like AT&T, GM, and most banks are blanketing the market, issuing pre-approved cards to almost anyone with an address and an income over fifteen thousand dollars a year, Cawley's approach is more selective. One-third of all the doctors in the United States, 20 percent of all lawyers, and half the American Dental Association carry his cards.

The average income of MBNA's Cardholders is fifty-four thousand dollars, far above the average for all bank cardholders. More than half pay the forty dollars for gold-card privileges. The other half pay the regular twenty dollars a year. In the credit-card industry as a whole, only 18 percent of cardholders pay premium fees, and many pay no fee at all.

Charging its customers interest that works out to an average of about 17 percent, the company earns $600 million a year.

Offering no rebates and no other particular trimmings other than you get with any other bank card, one wonders why the plan attracts so many professional people.

Charles Cawley claims he competes on service, not price. MBNA's customer-service line is answered by humans, not computers, and the switchboard is open twenty-four hours a day. Humans, not computers, review credit applications.

"The human touch is more expensive," Cawley says, "but it pays off in customer loyalty."

Well, not always. In 1992, Marine Midland Bank won the endorsement of the 280,000-member American Institute of Certified Public Accountants, a major loss for MBNA. Marine Midland offered the accountants a no-fee annual card. Cawley would not budge on its fee policy. Furthermore, MBNA executives point out that accountants, possessing an obvious cunning when it comes to money, virtually always pay their bills on time. This means, of course, that Marine Midland is giving free cards to people who pay their bills promptly, avoiding interest charges. One wonders what the reasoning behind Marine Midland's offer could have been.

Should they have any problems, the accountants, of course, will have to talk to computers.

In early April of 1994, the RAM Research Corporation, a credit-card research firm based in Frederick, Maryland, completed a survey which showed that the average credit-card interest rate was 16.47 percent among the banks, thrifts, and credit unions that issue Visa, MasterCard, Discover, and Optima credit cards.

In two years, the RAM Survey reported, the average card-interest rate has fallen almost 2 percent from 18.13 percent.

That broke the previous all-time low of 16.89 percent in 1978, said RAM President Robert McKinley.

David Brancoli, spokesman for Visa, gave the reason for the decline. "Competition," he said. "The market is competitive as hell."

"Competition," yes, but low prime rate, too. The rates are tied to the prime so when that goes up, so will credit-card interest. In six months in 1994, the prime rate went from 6 to 7.7 percent, and most credit-card rates were adjusted accordingly.

A number of organizations distribute listings of banks offering low-interest rates on credit cards, charging a small fee for the list. The Ram Corporation and Bank Cardholders of Washington, D.C., are two of them. Probably the most comprehensive chart and list is available from the Nilson Report, headquartered in Oxnard, California.

A recent *Wall Street Journal* article bemoaned the lowering of interest rates on credit cards suggesting that the "era of lush profits ends as card issuers face increased competition, savvy users."

"The gravy train is over," Merrill Lynch analyst Judah Kraushaar was quoted as saying.

The article went on to declare that the low rates being offered, most notably by the smaller banks, have forced the major bank issuers to lower their rates. Some have and, as previously noted, some have not. Those that have, have generally increased "penalty" fees to pick up some of the loss. The rest will be more than covered by the huge increases in volume. Bank-card spending in the first quarter of 1994 in the United States was up 26.2 percent. The total number of bank cards in circulation by the end of the quarter increased by 40.7 million, up 15 percent. The growth outside the U.S. was, without question, even greater at this writing.

Most credit-card charges are made on cards issued by the major banks, and, as noted, most major banks still charge near-usurious interest rates ranging from 16 to 20 percent. Some disguise this with those introductory rates that are considerably lower but jump in anywhere from three to twelve months. And remember, during the sorting-out period—the first two decades or so of bank credit cards—when they were making costly mistakes, they were nearly all charging up around 20 percent in annual interest. Neither Merrill Lynch nor the *Wall Street Journal* need shed tears. One wonders whether such expressions of gloom regarding bank profits were just innocent ignorance of facts or a desire not to make the greedy look too greedy.

By and large, Wall Street doesn't share any pessimism regarding bank cards. First USA, for example, is a Dallas company that Mr. Kraushaar's company, Merrill Lynch, helped go public in May, 1992. Through a Delaware bank subsidiary of the same name, it is basically only in the business of issuing credit cards. It ranks among the top fifteen U.S. credit-card issuers, and analysts have predicted that profits will rise by fifty-two million dollars annually after 1997.

First USA is selling at a price-earnings ratio of thirty-seven in a market where a twelve to fifteen price-earnings ratio is considered admirable. The "gravy train" is apparently still under a full head of steam, as further confirmed by a Federal Reserve study conducted by economist Lawrence M. Ausubol, who concluded that bank credit-card operations earn three to five times the rate of return earned by the banking industry at large.

An American Express survey in this period found that 37 percent of bank cardholders either canceled a card or signed up for another one in the past year, up from 31 percent one year earlier.

Certainly, the high-profile, co-branding companies had to have a great deal to do with any jump in the move from one card to another or the request for additional cards. One suspects, however, that most of the action is coming from people getting additional cards.

Have the major bank issuers been hurt by banks such as Wachovia and Arkansas Federal offering low interest rates? Well, the *Nilson Report* states that the top ten bank-card issuers accounted for 43 percent of outstanding credit-card balances in 1988 and 52 percent in 1994.

They may be making less on each dollar, but they're making a lot more dollars according to Robert Hammer, the credit-card analyst considered to be one of the most knowledgeable people in the industry.

To be precise, Hammer's research indicates that U.S. banks in 1993 had a profit of more than six billion dollars from credit-card operations or a stunning seventy dollars a year profit from each account. (Many accounts have more than one card.) With volume soaring, one would suspect that this figure, as well, will continue to increase dramatically.

The world's third largest credit-card market, after the United States and China, is Japan. Interestingly, despite the country's strong nationalistic tendencies, Visa and MasterCard have more cardholders in Japan than its own homegrown credit-card plan, JCB (the Japan Credit Bureau).

Visa leads with 44.9 million members. JCB, founded in 1988, has 27.9 million people carrying its cards.

In promotions to both members and merchants, the Japanese company emphasizes services rather than gimmicks, playing up ticket-buying faculties, travel arrangements, and cards for the middle-aged, the young, and the JCB ladies card which "provides special privileges and services to meet the needs of women cardmembers." The latter card probably would be deemed politically incorrect in the U.S.

The JCB cardholder is somewhat different than his American counterpart. The holder uses the card mostly in shops and department stores, draws fewer cash advances, and pays his bills more promptly.

The plan itself differs little from Visa or MasterCard except in the number and scope of services and the fewer number of merchants at which JCB members can charge. Interest rates are pegged at prime rate plus 8.5 percent, currently 15.75 percent.

Recently, JCB entered into an agreement with Household Bank to issue JCB cards on the mainland of the U.S., primarily, one would assume, to people who do business with and travel extensively to Japan.

Far behind both Visa and MasterCard in number of cardholders, charge volume, and merchant outlets is the Discover card with 40.6 million cardholders, all in the U.S. Volume is estimated at around 25 billion dollars for 1993.

The Discover card was founded in 1986 by Sears, Roebuck and Company with the then-unusual premise that there would be no fee and that customers charging more than three thousand dollars a year would earn a 1 percent cash rebate. The interest rate varies, depending on your use of the card. If you charge more than one thousand dollars a year, your rate for the subsequent year is prime plus 8.9 percent, 16.15 percent at this writing. For lesser users it goes to 19.80 percent. The industry-researched volume and cardholder figures (not disclosed by Discover) indicate cardholder usage is by far the lowest in the credit-card industry, slightly more than six hundred dollars a year. The card can also be used at some fifty-five thousand ATMs with an interest of 19.80 percent plus a transaction fee for cash advances ranging to 2.5 percent.

Discover was spun off to Dean Witter, a Sears subsidiary, in 1993 and is now a separate public company known as Dean Witter Discover.

Assuming that Discover cardholders don't travel outside the United States, one wonders, now that Citibank and other major issuers are dropping the annual membership fee, what Discover's appeal is. It has to be the 1 percent rebate, since the card is not accepted, even in the United States, at nearly as many outlets as Visa and MasterCard.

For years Discover and Visa slugged it out in court with Discover wanting to issue cards with the Visa imprint and cash in on the vast acceptance of that card. Visa argued that they were competitors and not entitled to such participation. A federal appeals court finally ruled in Visa's favor.

Simple arithmetic: someone carries a bank card with, for example, a 10 percent interest rate and pays $1,000 a year in interest. Low-interest cards usually charge a fee so add, let's say, $30 to that. Total: $1,030.00. The Discover Card member pays no membership fee but does pay more than $1,600 on a $10,000 average balance a year in interest before his rebate which is—$100.

Hey! Forty million Americans can't be wrong. Can they? Or are they merely just carrying another card?

Do credit-card companies who charge big interest rates make money? Discover, a free card with the lowest rate of use in the industry, showed net income of $319.7 million in 1993.

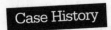

NUMBER SIX
ARNOLD—THE GAMBLER

Things were not going well at the 21 table for *Arnold. The dealer always seemed to draw one number higher than he did. If he drew nineteen, the dealer would turn up two picture cards and beat him with a twenty. He pulled twenty-one, with six cards, and the dealer pulled twenty-one, and he had to settle for a "push," which meant that he broke even. He had come to the table with six thousand dollars, fifty-eight hundred more than he'd told his wife he had with them when they arrived at the Desert Inn in Las Vegas that morning. "I swear," he'd told her before they'd left Denver, "I swear that I'll blow the two hundred dollars, we'll see some great shows, have some good dinners, and come home. It'll be a great weekend."

Rose was justifiably dubious. He'd gambled on their honeymoon and hadn't stopped until they went broke three years later; poker, gin rummy, horses—he'd bet on anything. But 21 was his game. That's what he always told her. Now, things had gotten better and he hadn't gambled for nearly two years. "I'm a new man," he told her. "I can take gambling or leave it." She wanted them to go to Aspen or maybe even L.A. to celebrate their fifth anniversary, but he'd talked her into Vegas, promising that he'd play some 21, just to prove he could stop, and his limit was two hundred dollars.

Now, Rose was in the health club getting a massage, a facial—the works. He was at a 21 table, and the six thousand dollars was rapidly disappearing. He moved to different tables several times to try to get his luck to change. Now he was down to his last two black chips—two hundred dollars. The dealer turned up a ten, suggesting he could well have twenty when he turned over his hidden card. Arnold stared at his cards again. A ten and a six. The dealer figured to beat him, needing a seven, eight, nine, or ten. Arnold tapped the table to indicate he wanted a card. The dealer dropped an open card in front of him—a six. He'd busted out. He'd lost the entire six thousand dollars. It almost didn't matter that the dealer turned up a six and busted himself when he drew an eight.

Arnold sat at the table numbly watching the other players rake in their winnings. One guy had stayed on twelve. "My God!" Arnold thought. "You don't have to know how to play this game to win."

He got up. He was disgusted and did what any other gambler would have done. He went out to the lobby, marched up to the money machine, pulled out his credit card, and got a cash advance of one thousand dollars.

In minutes he'd blown the thousand. Arnold made three more trips to the lobby, each time getting another thousand. He kept on losing. He was down to three hundred dollars. He'd now lost ninety-seven hundred dollars since he'd arrived in the casino that morning. He suddenly ignited.

Two hours later, at the same table, he was up thirty-six thousand dollars. It was pouring twenty-ones and twenties, and the dealer was coming up with seventeens and eighteens or busting out. Arnold was betting one thousand dollars on every hand, and sometimes he'd play two or three hands at one time. He was tossing out hundred-dollar tips to dealers and twenty-five dollars to cocktail waitresses.

But as in so many casino stories, Arnold's luck started to change again.

Faster than he'd won it, he gave it back. He doubled up elevens and pull twos or split eights and pull sevens. In less than an hour he was down to two hundred dollars—the exact amount he'd told Rose he'd brought. He pushed it out, and the dealer dealt. He had two kings. The dealer turned up a three, then an eight, and a queen for 21. He looked at the money as the dealer swept it away. Suddenly, Rose was at his side looking pretty and happy and healthy.

"How'd you do?" she asked.

He shrugged. "Well," he said, "I'm through for the trip. I blew the two hundred dollars."

Chapter Fifteen

THE CREDIT CARDS FOR PEOPLE WHO CAN'T GET CREDIT CARDS

A DECADE OR SO before Frank MacNamara's wonderful little card came to be, the Flatbush National Bank in Brooklyn issued certificates to bank depositors that could be redeemed at local shops. When returned to the bank by the merchants, the bank paid for the purchases and deducted the amount on the certificate from the depositor's account, taking a substantial cut from both storekeeper and customer for their efforts.

It was costly and cumbersome and with slow hand-billing, didn't have much appeal to either merchant or customer and was discontinued well before the Diners Club was born.

But in a sense, it was the predecessor, not to the credit card or the charge card, but to the debit card.

Debit cards, a surefire money-maker for the banks, are used primarily by people who can't qualify for a bank card, either because they have a bad credit rating or no credit rating or, perhaps, because they've not paid their credit-card bills on time in the past and are persona non grata at the various credit departments. Some people can't get credit cards because their income doesn't meet the industry's standards, which themselves are pretty low, usually fifteen thousand dollars a year for bank cards.

Some who use the debit cards are simply wiser than most of us and realize that a credit card can be an invitation to spend beyond one's limits and want to put some controls on themselves and/or their spouses.

The procedure is quite simple. It's like the Flatbush Bank did it, only with computers. You deposit a set amount in the bank, get your card, and charge against it. The computer that accepts your card and the information on the magnetic tape on the card enable the bank to record each transaction and to deduct the purchase from your deposit.

ATM cards used at cash machines are a form of debit cards, and their use for charging for other than cash withdrawals has been expanding rapidly. The Visa (Interlink) and MasterCard (Maestro) debit cards are the same as their regular credit cards in that they're accepted at all Visa and MasterCard merchants. Many of the same merchants will also honor ATM cards.

Why do the banks like debit cards? No credit risks and the"float"—with a credit card a customer doesn't have to pay his bill for twenty-five days to avoid interest charges, and the bank, which is paying for his purchases almost daily, is actually lending him money for that period at no interest. On the other hand, debit-card purchase is repaid to the bank immediately. Any unused portion of the deposit just sits there accruing income to the bank much like a traveler's check. And there's that third big reason—paper work. That banker's dream, a "less-check" society. Last year U.S. banks handled fifty-five billion checks at what they claim was a cost of $1.30 per check. With a debit card, there are no checks, not even one a month to pay your monthly statement. As in the case of a recorded credit-card charge, the cost to the bank is estimated at fifteen cents a blip, one blip to a transaction. Since the bank isn't loaning you money, you pay no interest, but the bank always has your money, and they're not paying you interest either.

The wisdom of using debit cards should not be minimized, particularly to people who have limited finances or a tendency to spend more than they've got or may get. *American Banker*'s Jeff Kutler thinks home-banking services and interactive television/home shopping will result in a sharp increase in the use of debit cards both at the bank's urging and through general education of the consumer who more and more has right in his own home the dangerous invitation to financial suicide through overuse of credit cards. Kutler says, "Younger people, especially, generally don't have thousands of dollars of credit lines and view debit cards as a clean and convenient alternative for everyday transactions."

Visa has 74.5 million Interlink debit cards in circulation around the world. MasterCard, with its emphasis on blue-collar customers, is even stronger with this plan. It has 110 million cardholders in its Maestro system. Industry analysts figure that the debit cardholder, after having the card for three years, reflects a forty-six dollars per year profit for the issuing bank.

In 1993, there were twelve U.S. banks including Citibank, Bank of America, Chemical, Chase Manhattan, and Home Savings who were each holding at least twenty billion dollars in debit-card deposits.

If you aren't quite sure that's a bonanza, think of the secured card which is for real losers, people with a miserable credit standing. You get, let us say, a secured card with a five-hundred-dollar limit, but you have to put up a deposit of five hundred dollars that is not used but on which you draw interest at most banks, of let's say 5 percent. You pay a fee for the card, say twenty-five dollars per year, and you pay a high interest rate, perhaps 19 percent on your purchases when you exceed the twenty-five day interest-free limit. Unlike the debit card, purchases are not deducted from your deposit. It just sits there as collateral on your charges which can't exceed that collateral.

In essence, the bank is *loaning you your own money* at a rate of 14 percent (your 5 percent interest less the 19 percent bank interest charge) and charging you an annual fee for it. Some issuers, Bank of America for example, are even more onerous, charging 19.80 percent interest and paying you only two percent on your security deposit. So, you're paying 17 percent to borrow your own money. But, hey, you're the idiot with a lousy credit history who's "got to have a credit card."

Before anyone gets too heated on this subject, it's worth mentioning that there are only a million or so secured cards out in the U.S., a mere speck on the overall card scene. It also should be noted that some banks will allow a secured cardholder to upgrade to a debit card after a year or so of good credit experience.

Even with security in hand, banks often have bad debt losses from cardholders who exceed their limits before the computers catch up with them. In 1992, secured-card losses were figured to be slightly over 1 percent with bad-debt losses on regular bank cards at 4.3 percent. Improving computer techniques are quickly putting an end to that problem.

In mid-1994, banks started to make secured cards more competitive, realizing that charging people for using their own money was a business that should be encouraged. Led by Citibank, Wells Fargo, Bank of America, and Sanwa Bank, rates were cut, in some cases, to 15.9 percent. Annual fees were lowered to eighteen dollars or waived for those with checking overdraft protection linked to the credit card.

Robert McKinley, in *CardTrak*, the credit-card newsletter put out by the RAM Corporation, said that, "Credit cards issuers know they've got to reach out to new markets if they want to continue to grow. The market is so saturated that issuers are turning over rocks looking for customers." Apparently, this market, comprising mostly people with past bankruptcies or payment problems, is under another upturned rock.

Citibank says 70 percent of its secured cardholders prove to be so reliable about paying their bills they "graduate" to ordinary unsecured cards in less than two years. This means, we assume, that 30 percent of these cardholders are having various degrees of difficulty in paying their bills.

But even at 1 percent, it's a helluva business, and the number of people with bad credit, really bad credit, who really want credit cards, is growing all the time.

Chapter Sixteen

AMEX, DINERS AND THE DISAPPEARING CREDIT CARD COMPANY

AMERICAN EXPRESS, rapidly being outdistanced, doesn't want its card to be known only as a businessman's card, but basically, it is.

Let's face it, Amex sells prestige. You carry an Amex card—a gold card or a platinum card—and it marks you as an affluent business and traveling person. Flash the Visa card and essentially, you're a tourist.

An image of affluence is hardly needed at your local supermarket or K-Mart, but it could come in handy at the George V Hotel in Paris or even at the ticket counter of a major airline. The world is image conscious, and American Express spends more money ($210 million a year, about the same as Visa and Citibank combined) to advertise and embellish its credit-card image than anyone else.

The bank cards are honored at more establishments and for more services, and they charge merchants a lower service fee, although Amex is gradually lowering its to be competitive. Because of the lower fee, some stores and restaurants openly show their preference for the bank cards. They're being shortsighted. One of the important tools we used to sell the Diners Club in the early days of the credit card was the survey that showed the businessmen, who were basically the Diners Club membership, spent more at a restaurant than cash customers.

The same holds true for Amex members as compared to bank cardholders. They spend more. In 1993, the average Visa member charged $2,646, the Master-Card member, $2,088. The average American Express member's charges for the year were $3,510. Diners Club average spending was $3,281 per cardholder.

Why? Essentially because most Visa and MasterCard charges are paid for by the cardholder, and most Amex and Diners Club charges are paid for by a corporation or are charged off as tax-deductible business expenses by the individual.

There's another explanation. The American Express and Diners cardholders are more affluent. They've got more money and spend more money. They travel more and dine out more often, more business lunches and customer wine and dining.

The magic word in the life of a big public company is "growth." There's a desperate urgency to show your stockholders that you're not only the same good old, solid company that has made huge profits forever but that you're a "growth" company. After all, why should someone buy your stock if you're still only great. The object is to be greater. In the life of a public-company executive, the object is to get the price of your stock up.

American Express has a good thing going for it in its card primarily for travelers and business people. Eighty-five percent of the seventy-one thousand Amex employees are involved with credit cards one way or the other. Credit cards are no longer the tail that wags the dog. It's really the whole dog. It has succeeded because it has convinced the travel and entertainment crowd that it's the card for those who require prestige and are willing to pay a little extra for it.

When they have failed it has been because, in the battle for growth and dominance, they have tried to compete with the bank cards and can't.

In 1987, Amex introduced the Optima card. In a sense, it was the bank card for American Express card-holders, a revolving-credit plan. What it really was a departure from the unwritten dictum, if you can carry an Amex card, you shouldn't need revolving credit. In its first two years, Optima made some small profits, then in 1991, net charge-offs for credit losses rose to an incredible 10 percent of the $4.5 billion in outstanding debt. The Optima program lost $146 million in one year.

The plan was completely overhauled. Tiered interest rates ranging from 12.5 percent up to 19.40 percent for marginal credit risks were instituted, but the marginal rate didn't apply to too many because the card was withdrawn from most who didn't appear to be financially solid.

Stronger monitoring procedures on cardholder spending were instituted, and, most importantly, solicitations for Optima cards were restricted to existing Amex cardholders for the problems had not come from the businessman who wanted prestige and could afford it. Credit standards had been lowered, and a shabbier crowd had moved into town.

In 1992, Amex issued 200,000 new Optima cards. In 1991, they had issued 1,000,000.

Just after Labor Day of 1994, American Express, apparently no longer suffering from a case of bad-debt jitters, announced they were launching yet another revolving-credit card. Stating that they had, after four thousand consumer interviews and other "intensive" research that included think tanks and concept groups, come up with the Optima True Grace card. A six-month promotional interest rate of 7.9 percent is being held up as an enticement. After that interest will jump to 8.75 percentage points over prime. Cardholders who use the card three times a year will pay no membership fee.

If the cardholder has more than three late payments in a six-month period, their interest rate will jump to more than 21 percent.

So far, there's nothing that isn't being offered by dozens of banks using the Visa and MasterCard system. What's the gimmick?

Well, "True Grace" is the gimmick. Unlike many of the credit-card issuers, but certainly not all, interest won't be charged until twenty-five days after the close of each monthly account cycle, even if the cardholder carries over the balance.

Philip Reise, the president of American Express' Cardholder Services, projects a million users for the card within six months. He also says that the company plans to launch another new credit card early in 1995 and more soon after.

So, they're feet first into revolving credit, once again. Harvey Golub, Amex's chairman says further that he expects credit card (revolving) receivables to reach thirty billion dollars by the year 2,000. If it does, it would give Amex its first substantial gains in years.

But it won't.

Once again, the desperate need for "growth," to satisfy investors and analysts and to rationalize big executive bonuses and salaries, is pushing a company into something it probably shouldn't do.

Some in the industry felt that Amex was striking back because Visa (particularly) and MasterCard (somewhat) are making a big run for corporate business. Some aren't quite sure why they went this route. Even Amex executive Frank Skillern admitted to *Time* magazine, "The world probably doesn't need a new credit card."

The "world" might very well be agreeing. A month or so after introducing "True Grace," American Express announced that it was reorganizing its credit-card operations, cutting six thousand jobs in the process.

Amex will probably be more selective about who it gives the cards to than it was with just plain Optima. "The first time didn't work out so well," John J. Byrne, a former American Express director stated. "I think Harvey will be very careful this time."

Philip Reise echoed that feeling of wariness. "Some people say that good judgment comes from bad experience. If that is true, we now have very good judgment."

One would think that all the research might have come up with something better. "True Grace" isn't exactly on par with Amex's "Do you know this man?" campaign. One wonders if simply offering an interest rate which would have saved the cardholder a great deal more money wouldn't have been a simpler and more enticing sell.

Good ideas, nevertheless, are still in the mix. Sticking to the corporate-business image, the company has introduced the corporate-purchasing card. Its purpose is to offer a billing and purchasing service for member office expenses and to sharply reduce paperwork and general overhead and, through consolidated purchasing, even offer lower prices on merchandise. According to *Credit Card Management* magazine, Amex has entered a $300-billion market. Diners Club's Bob Rosseau is even more optimistic on the subject of corporate purchasing, predicting that all credit-card charges for business procurement will be in the area of $500 to $600 billion by the year 2000.

Unlike the decision to compete with the bank cards and offer revolving credit, it's a terrific plan. An Ernst and Young study revealed that it typically costs a corporation up to one hundred dollars to process one purchasing transaction even if the item is a ten-dollar stapler. The American Express billing system, unlike the banks, offers country-club billing (a copy of signed receipts) with its monthly bills. This gives a company the individual receipts it needs for office purchases. There are reports that Amex may be ditching country-club billing, just as Diners Club did years ago. They've already discontinued it to Canadian members. At any rate, the corporate purchasing plan is a good one, and it's a road one would think American Express would continue to travel. Their principal problem in traversing it might be that the banks, once their greatest ally, constitute the most important source of marketing and sales help for such a program and are now their arch rivals.

Not to be outdone in the gimmick department, both American Express and Diners Club have mileage plans not unlike Citibank's Aadvantage and other such programs offered by banks. All are now starting to pile hotel-room charges and other credit-card uses on to their offers, and you can now get free air mileage, hotel accommodations, and other gifts if you use their card often enough.

"We're going to continue to try to expand into charges for personal, as well as business, needs," an Amex representative told me. "We've added K-Mart and Wal-Mart as part of that expansion."

If American Express exists primarily because it's a status credit card, K-Mart and Wal-Mart will hardly add to that status.

"I'm gonna go with the horse that brung me," the old chestnut goes.

The horse that "brung" American Express this far in the credit-card business is snob appeal. The best TV commercials they ever ran were those that showed famous and important people with their Amex cards.

It has brought them far—35.4 million cardholders in 1993 with a charge volume of $124.06 billion. Revenues from merchant discounts and cardholder fees were $5.48 billion. Not up to Visa's $542.2 billion in charges or 333.1 million cardholders but, of course, Visa is an association of a whole lot of companies, and American Express is only one.

American Express' green or personal card, as it's called, comes with an annual membership fee of $55, the gold card, $75 and the platinum card, $300. Among the many things a platinum card will bring you abroad are emergency transaction and free medical evacuation coverage should you become dangerously ill and have to be flown home in an ambulance-plane.

Three hundred dollars for a credit card. What memories that evokes of those arguments with Frank MacNamara over whether anybody would be willing to actually pay for a credit card. Then followed our anguish over whether to charge three dollars or five and our decision to go with the lesser figure purely because we thought we might lose all our cardholders if we were too greedy.

You get all sorts of things with your gold and platinum cards just as you get all sorts of pluses with Visa or MasterCard Gold. The most notable might be very high credit limits.

It should be remembered that although American Express advertises that, unlike the bank cards, they have no credit limits, accounts are monitored, and there are limits depending on one's credit worthiness. Gold and, particularly, platinum cardholders have higher internal limits. They also can get cash, a lot of cash, when they need it, and for businessmen who travel this still can be important. Green card members can draw one thousand dollars in a seven-day period from American Express offices around the world. For the most part, the money is debited against the member's bank account as though a check had been drawn. Some gold and many platinum cardholders can draw cash and just repay it on their monthly bill; gold, twenty-five hundred dollars within seven days and platinum, ten thousand dollars in a thirty-day period.

There are also special perks for the crème de la crème—various insurance policies, reservations, problem solvers for travelers in trouble. "Highly personalized services," Amex calls them, "for our affluent, high-spending members."

And it's that kind of verbiage that has made American Express what it is. Who among us would not like to be treated as if we were among the "affluent" and "high spending"?

"Rent the yacht in Cannes, Miranda, and call the Aga Kahn for dinner. And polish up my platinum card."

The fee for the Optima Card is a lowly fifteen dollars for those who are already American Express members, twenty-five dollars for those who are not.

Hardly, a prestigious annual membership fee for the affluent these days.

But, American Express tells us, Optima (Optima True Grace) will be important—much more important.

Maybe. But I don't think so.

TRS, the name for American Express' Travel Related Services Division, earned $895 million in 1993, the largest part of that coming from credit cards, the rest, basically, from their traveler's cheques and travel agencies. Their 35.4 million credit cards indicate a small increase, but even that is misleading. The gain, which came in the face of huge increases for the bank cards and after several years of losses in the number of Amex cardholders, would have actually been another drop in membership had not the U.S. government switched to Amex some 900,000 employees who had been holding federally funded Diners Club credit cards for as long as ten years.

It was that "growth" thing again. In that respect it was a bonanza to American Express who had 36.6 million cardholders in 1991, dropped to 34.7 in 1992, and would have declined to 34.5 in 1993 had it not been for the switch.

Looking good to stockholders aside, the Amex decreases these past years were slight, and, as indicated, the credit-card operation is still highly profitable. And remembering again that Visa and MasterCard are associations and not card issuers, American Express trails only Discover and Citibank as far as having the most cardholders, but Amex cardholders all pay for their cards and are charged a lot more. None of Discover's do and, now as reported, most of the fees for Citibank's members are being phased out. It's not difficult to get people to take your card for nothing. That's another reason the American Express cardholder uses his card more frequently. Again, as we discovered in 1950, you pay for it, you use it.

But the rub in the corporate offices at American Express remains "growth." They have a strong, healthy card system. It makes a lot of money, and it's the most prestigious major credit card in the world—but where's the "growth"?

For years they tried to get those 900,000 federal government cardholders away from the Diners Club. When they finally succeeded, American Express insisted that the government's General Services Administration switched because research indicated that their cardholders would get better service if they made the change; that Amex travel offices and other personal services could not be matched by the Diners Club.

There were other considerations.

After several years of discussions, Diners Club felt it could do no more to keep the account than they had done to get it, waive all membership fees for the 900,000 cardholders. American Express, faced with another year of decline, went all out. They would pay, *pay* the U.S. government to replace the Diners Club cards with Amex. To be precise, they would and did pay twenty dollars a card, a total of eighteen million dollars, for the biggest single account in the credit-card world. When the switch remained uncertain, American Express threw in another one hundred million dollars or so in down-the-line rebates based on volume.

The deal was made, and American Express promptly announced it had "growth."

Late in 1993, Diners Club U.S. membership, which had been 7.3 million, shrunk to 6.4 million, the lost constituting the exact number of government cardholders that went to Amex.

Average spending for the first quarter of 1994 had, however, an interesting reversal. American Express, proud possessor of those 900,000 new cardholders, saw a slight drop from its 1993 average spending by individual cardholders while Diners Club, whose membership base shrank drastically, saw an increase. It seems that only one of three federal government employees use their credit card in any one month, and of those that do, one-third do not settle until accounts are at least sixty days past due.

One might conclude that, with no fee, rebates, late payments, and low spending per card, the 900,000 acquisition by American Express was not a high-profit take-over.

Diners Club worldwide charge volume in 1993 was $20.81 billion, a far cry from the single digit millions we crowed over in the early 1950s but only 2.03 percent of the year's general-purpose credit-card total. It is fifth in any listing of the five major worldwide credit cards (Carte Blanche isn't even thought about), trailing JCB by $12 billion and American Express by a little less than $104 billion. Visa and MasterCard, of course, are out of sight, but the Diners Club keeps plugging along, emphasizing its basic service as a businessman's card, charging an industry-high $80 a card for individual cards. (They have no gold, platinum, sapphire, or plutonium cards.)

Their target is the corporation, and the membership fee drops to thirty dollars a card if the company has from one to twenty-four cardholders, descends further to twenty-five dollars for membership numbering from twenty-five to ninety-nine, and plummets to five dollars a card for companies holding more than five thousand cards. One assumes that if you have 900,000 cardholders lying around, they'll once again waive the fee altogether.

For an extra fee, forty dollars per card, members can participate in the true rewards program, earning air travel miles and an assortment of additional prizes ranging from a pair of binoculars to vacations in lush resort hotels.

Like all other systems, the Diners Club card can be used to withdraw cash from automatic teller machines. There are 127,000 around the world that will accept the card. Unlike many of the others, the withdrawal is not immediately deducted from the cardholder's bank account, and there is no interest charge. There is, however, a four-percent service charge for each transaction, not unlike the charge for similar service imposed by some competitors, some of whom also charge interest from day one of the withdrawal.

The Diners Club is big on sending you paper. They flood their members with mail-order pitches and a constant flow of information that reminds you that membership offers you such benefits as a $350,000 travel accident policy, $1,250 coverage on lost baggage, car rental insurance, and twenty-four hour traveler's aid. Unfortunately, most of the other credit cards offer just about the same thing.

As Amex has, Diners Club is forging into corporate purchasing, offering mass-buying service, account supervisors for large companies, and, of course, capital. They will, like any other service, carry charges for at least thirty days and have shown no reluctance to advance monies to solidify relationships. Bob Rosseau talks of "a billion dollars a year in charges" from one company like Northrop. A corporate purchasing deal, he enthuses, that would include the purchasing of equipment and, indeed, even airplane parts on a Diners Club card. The discussions of such a deal are already underway, he says.

What the Diners Club offers is good service and excellent charge coverage outside the United States. More than 11 billion of that $20.81 billion Diners Club charge volume in 1993 was beyond U.S. borders, and the card is more eagerly accepted in foreign countries than it is in the country in which it and the credit card was born.

The reason for such acceptance is elementary. Remember, when the Diners Club was founded, only the operations in the U.S. and Canada were kept. The rest of the world was franchised and operated by local businessmen who had stronger contacts and a better understanding of how to deal with merchants in their homeland. Citibank has, in recent years, bought part or all of 15 of those 175 franchises. Most interestingly, only 1.3 million of the 6.4 million Diners cardholders are U.S. citizens, making it a truly international card.

It would seem that, unlike American Express, Diners Club has no plans to attempt to win over the general consumer. "We take care of business" is their slogan. It's a good one and a wise one. They are, in a sense, a boutique credit-card company, specializing in the needs of business people (particularly business people who travel out of their own country) and pretty much ignoring the K-Mart crowd.

Well, they're owned by Citibank, the biggest issuer of bank cards in the world. Why *would they* compete with the mother company? More importantly, they *can't* compete with Citibank and Visa and MasterCard in dealing with the family that goes to K-Mart any more than American Express can.

They are where we were when we started in the 1950s—issuing a card for business people with good credit ratings, charging for the card, offering prestige and service, and trying to stay out of trouble.

Carte Blanche still exists—barely. I am told that it has become merely a list and a telephone. New memberships are not solicited. If a new member application does come in, there is no credit department, so it's sent over to the Diners Club, its Citibank brother. The Diners Club credit department checks it out and, if approved, a card is issued. Why anyone would want the card, other than to save it for posterity, is suspect. Carte Blanche, Barron Hilton's dream which never really got off the ground, sits in reserve at Citibank.

Case History   **NUMBER SEVEN**
ERIC—THE GOURMET

*Eric Bonor was one of the first big Diners Club credit problems. Joe Titus solemnly reported to us at an executive meeting one morning that Eric's card has been used on one of the oddest spending sprees ever seen; one that lasted only three days but had accumulated more than five thousand dollars in charges and was limited only to food and drink except for one car-rental charge.

Eric, Joe informed us, was a very wealthy man, and the six thousand dollars was not a problem, except that he had called the Diners Club, upon receipt of his bill, eventually been connected with Titus, and told Joe that not only hadn't he used his card for the charges in question but that he was in the hospital for minor surgery during the questioned period.

Joe's investigators followed up. Hertz had accepted the card for rental of a car and that meant the user of the card had to show his driver's license, but Bonor told them that only his Diners Club card was missing. The Hertz rental form confirmed that the driver's license presented had borne Eric's name.

The investigators checked with the hospital and confirmed his three-day stay.

A six thousand dollar write-off in the fifties was comparable to one ten times that amount in today's high-ticket economy. We were not happy about the probability of writing off the charges. Word of the imminent loss was all over the credit department.

"Say," said one of the credit people as he walked into Joe Titus's office with a Diners Club application, "isn't this the same guy whose card was used for the six grand?"

Titus took the application. It bore the name Eric Bonor. Bonor's existing credit-card file was on his desk. He compared the original application with the new one. One gave Bonor's age as fifty-two, and the new one listed it as twenty-four. There were differences in jobs and bank accounts—but the address was the same. Titus grinned.

Eric Bonor, Jr., had "borrowed" his father's credit card during Sr.'s three-day hospital stay and gone on a binge that probably remains unparalleled in credit-card annals in the singularity of the purchases involved. In the three days, he'd rented the car and returned it seventy-two hours later. During that time, all his other charges were in New York's finest restaurants. It was a veritable moving feast, a bacchanal. He later recalled that at least thirty people were involved at different times. He had charged for more than a hundred breakfasts, lunches, dinners, and late-night suppers at seventeen different restaurants. He had eaten lustily at all seventeen. The meals included steak dinners at Manny Wolf's and Chandler's, elegant dinners at Chambord and Voisin, huge Italian dinners, smorgasbord feasts, breakfast at Reubens, and smart lunches at the Algonquin.

It was a weekend for the gourmet and gourmand, and Eric Bonor, Jr., appeared to be both. Examination of the restaurant bills showed that the fine wines and champagne had flowed like—fine wines and champagne should.

Eric Bonor, Sr., and Jr. showed up at Joe Titus's office the next day. Both were large men in the 250-pound weight range. Titus dutifully reported afterward that Jr. had gas and looked bloated.

Sr. was somewhat embarrassed. Jr. was contrite. Sr. paid the bill. Jr.'s application for a Diners Club card was rejected.

Chapter Seventeen

HOW MANY
IS TOO MANY?

EVER SINCE THE credit card was created, but particularly since the introduction of the bank card and easy access to revolving credit, critics have been warning that giving people a blank check is the fiscal equivalent of handing many of them a loaded revolver with the suggestion that Russian roulette can help clear your sinuses.

The credit-card companies point out that there have long been numerous safeguards against runaway spending: those applying for credit cards are checked out and potential nonpayers (people who would most likely overspend) are rejected. Cardholders are given limits which reflect income, net worth, and paying habits. When those limits are reached or exceeded, computers set off warning signals. Credit bureaus look for people applying for an inordinate numbers of cards. Penalties for late payments and for those who exceed their current limits serve as warnings to cardholders, telling them to use caution.

Some of the above is true. Most are not, except in the case of the smaller banks which charge realistically lower interest rates and thus can't absorb higher credit losses.

In 1993 bank-card issuers in the United States wrote off bad debts of 4.3 percent of their total volume, approximately seventeen billion dollars. Actually, it was a pretty good year. In 1992, bad-debt write-offs were at 5.8 percent. They came down primarily because the recession and unemployment eased in 1993.

If the same 4.3 percent held for all-purpose cards for the entire world, credit losses would have been forty-three billion dollars. That, however, is not the case. Outside of the United States and Canada and Great Britain, where losses run about the same as in the U.S., most cards are debit cards and, it is estimated that losses on those run as low as .8 percent depending on the country, the paying habits of its inhabitants, and the stringencies of its bank laws.

In France, for example, a personal identification number is required with nearly all charges. Losses are primarily from fraud and computer foul-up and from delays in posting charges, since debit cards are designed to effect changes against predeposited funds. Also, bad debts for American Express and Diners Club are substantially lower than those for bank cards.

American Express is secretive about its credit losses, but experts estimate that they run about 2.5 percent of charge volume, and without its Optima Card that figure would be lower. Diners Club, so dominantly into corporate cards, says its losses are now 1.02 percent of total volume, a figure not seen since the early days of the industry. Revolving credit, it seems, is the principal demon that creates excessive bad debt.

If 4.3 percent of all bank charges result in bad debt, they are only part of the approximately 17 percent of all charges that are paid late each month.

That means an awful lot of people are having a tough time paying their bills.

From a booklet titled "Building Your Credit Knowledge," issued by some banks to perspective cardholders who have been rejected for any of various reasons:

"If your application was denied because of 'Sufficient Revolving Credit,' it suggests you already have multiple credit-card accounts. Regardless of what you may owe on these other credit cards, we calculate your monthly obligations based upon the total of all credit limits (or lines), not your outstanding balance. So, say you have three credit cards, each with a $2,000 limit. Your monthly obligations would be based upon $6,000, not the current balance on your accounts."

We decided to see how tough it is for a marginal credit risk to get a credit card—to get a number of credit cards.

The best known collector of credit cards is a fifty-year-old Californian by the name of Walter Cavanagh. Eighteen years ago, he owned just one card. Then he made a bet with a friend to see who could collect the most credit cards in a year. He won with 143 cards. The prize was dinner, and his friend paid with plastic.

At this writing, he has 1,262 active cards, a figure that grows at the rate of one or two cards a week. He has been rejected for a credit card only once, by a store that suggested he already had too much credit.

The limits on his cards would grant him the right to charge *$1.6 million.* He actually uses them very conservatively, paying off any charges promptly each month and carrying only two or three cards with him at a time.

But Walter Cavanagh is in the *Guinness Book of Records,* and he's not your ordinary cardholder. Let's assume he's got a great credit rating and deserves to be the holder of 1,262 credit cards. What about someone who's marginal or, perhaps, even less than marginal?

I asked a friend of mine who we'll call *Al, because that's not his name, to help me out. Al is a screenwriter—an unemployed screenwriter. He hasn't sold a script or had any kind of real employment since 1991. He's in his sixties, and his hopes for a bonanza somewhere down the line get dimmer every day. He's been married three times, and he has a nine-year-old child from his current marriage. His wife works as a part-time salesclerk.

The family lives primarily on a union pension, interest from some past investments, and equity which, little by little, gets smaller and smaller. Al has refinanced his house several times and drives a ten-year-old car he shares with his wife. He is frequently delinquent in paying bills but eventually manages to get them paid.

Al is a bright, talented guy who is simply having a tough time of it. He's had a Citibank MasterCard for years. It's usually charged right up to his ten-thousand-dollar limit, but he pays his monthly minimums. He is constantly the target of phone and mail pitches from other credit-card issuers.

Al ignored them until I asked him not to.

In a period of just over thirty days, he filled out a dozen credit-card applications; most of them having arrived in his mailbox unsolicited. When asked, he listed his annual income accurately at "$15,000 plus." In most cases, he wasn't even asked and was told he was "pre-approved," often because of his "outstanding credit record."

Here's what happened.

◆ Without supplying any financial information, he was given an AT&T Universal Visa card with a pre-approved credit line of $3,000 and no charge for the card forever. The service included the right to transfer balances from other credit cards at 11.9 percent interest.

◆ He got an Optima card from American Express which was pre-approved and required no additional financial information. The credit line was $2,000.

◆ Because his credit history was again so "outstanding," the limit on his Citibank MasterCard was extended, at his request, to $15,000.

◆ He received a pre-approved application from the Spiegel Catalogue Company which required only that he indicate his income bracket. He did and promptly received a card giving him a credit line of $825. This was not a bank card, merely an unsolicited in-house credit card.

◆ He filled out a pre-approved application for a Wells Fargo Preferred Aadvantage Gold card and received it within two weeks. His credit line was $7,600. He did not respond to an offer of an insurance policy which would pay his credit-card bill if he was ever unemployed, primarily because he was already unemployed.

◆ He applied for and got a Chemical Bank/Shell MasterCard with a credit line of $1,500. Once again, he was invited to transfer balances owed other credit-card companies at a rate of 10.95 percent. There was no annual fee for the first year or for each year thereafter if he made six purchases a year with his card.

◆ His nine-year-old son received an application for membership in Citibank Aadvantage which both he and his son decided to pass on.

◆ He was pre-approved for a GM Card (MasterCard), returned the invitation, and got the card, with a $5,000 credit line and a pitch to buy or lease a General Motors car or truck and earn a 5 percent rebate. Nowhere on the application or in the pitch was there a reference to an annual limit ($500) on the car-purchase rebate.

◆ He applied for a Visa card from AARP, the American Association of Retired People, of which he was a member. The application was detailed and among other things, asked for his income which he, as usual, listed as $15,000 plus and his present employer which he noted was "self" and occupation, "writer." He received his card with a credit line of $2,000.

◆ He returned a pre-approved pitch sent to him by the Automobile Club of California, no annual fee. A packet of checks with which he could transfer balances from other accounts came with the MasterCard card. Interest rate on them was 14.9 percent. His credit line: $2,000.

◆ He applied for and received a Chase Reward Consolidator with which he could transfer credit-card debts at an 11.9 percent interest rate. His credit line was set at $7,000.

He applied for two cards, a Gold Visa from Fleet Bank of Hartford, Connecticut, and a Visa from Arkansas Federal of Little Rock, Arkansas. Both banks offer among the lowest interest rates in the country. Neither rejected him but both sent along a request for copies of his last two years of personal tax returns.

Since he's had declared earnings of a little more than $16,000 in each year, he ignored the requests.

He now had, in addition to his original card, nine new credit-card accounts plus an increase on the credit limit on the card he'd already had. In all, his credit line was now $45,925, almost three times what his earnings had been for each of the preceding three or four years. Within thirty days after receiving the cards, he was solicited by five other credit-card issuers.

The average number of credit cards being held by Americans who have at least one card has been judged to be as high as eight. They include merchant credit cards as well as bank and t-and-e cards. It's estimated the holders of all-purpose cards carry an average of four.

There are only two reasons anyone needs four all-purpose credit cards or eight credit cards of any kind since the merchant or service that doesn't honor most all-purpose credit cards is getting rarer and rarer: you either want to collect them, as Walter Cavanagh does, or you want to charge more than you reasonably should and are spreading your debt around.

The documentation on these pages proves something we probably all believed anyway: almost anybody can get almost as many credit cards as they want. Once again the banks, displaying their largesse, keep filling the chambers of our fiscal revolvers with bullets. My friend Al returned all the cards he applied for except the one he'd held originally. "Things," he told me, "are rough enough."

Chapter Eighteen

ON SPENDING TOO MUCH

"Government has a function in encouraging banks not to lend money that will not be repaid, whether the borrower is a real-estate developer, a Third World country, a college student, or a day laborer."—Author Martin Meyer, *Wall Street Journal*, November 21, 1994

A 1991 POLL OF 2,000 companies conducted by the Kessler Exchange in Northridge, California, a consulting firm for small businesses, showed that 30 percent were relying more on personal credit cards because they were unable to get bank lines of credit or other loans.

"About 20 percent of all bankruptcies are business failures, and 80 percent personal," according to Paul Richard of the National Center for Financial Education. "But of that 80 percent, about 40 percent are the result of people trying to start their own businesses, usually using personal credit cards.

"Credit-card spending is such a part of the American culture," Richard says, "that people don't think about the real costs. Some people luck out and it pays off." —*Los Angeles Times,* June 6, 1993

Actor-director Robert Townsend on the making of his breakthrough film, *Hollywood Shuffle*: "It was easy to make a full-length film on credit cards. Catering the food, I'd go to the supermarket and charge all the chicken, potato chips, you name it. I couldn't pay people so I'd say, 'Actors, crew, who needs to fill up with gas?' Twenty cars would go over to the Shell station on my Visa.

"I was starving, but I had a forty-thousand-dollar credit line. I used the last of my credit to rent the Writers Guild screening room. I catered the wine, everything, on credit cards."—Bonnie Allen, *Essence* magazine, September, 1987

Director Richard Linklater on how he financed his first film, *Slacker*: "I got my first card in 1982. I had a steady job and was bringing in about twenty grand a year. It had a $3,500 credit limit. Eventually I received three others. One had a $3,500 credit limit, another $2,500, and a third $2,000. So I had an $11,500 credit line and I was still making twenty grand. I started to apply for others.

"I made *Slacker* with two Visas, two MasterCards, a Sear's card, a Foley's department store account, and Shell, Exxon and Mobil cards. The picture was a critical success, but I couldn't pay off the charges until a year or so after it opened, when I got an advance for writing and directing my next film [*Dazed and Confused*]. In the meantime, the card companies were relentless. When I finally paid them off, I still couldn't get a card, even though I was now working with major studios and making good money.

"Today I am a reformed member of the Five Percent Club." (He and friends understand that the credit-card companies write off approximately five percent of their volume.)

He now uses secured credit cards.—From an interview with Michael Simmons

"Credit cards give a poor man a chance—even a fleeting chance—to be a rich man. How bad can that be?" —Anonymous

"We issue credit cards to students, primarily college students. We have a small test that we're currently running in the high-school market. It consists of five thousand, college-bound, high-school seniors. We're trying to preempt the competition."—Michelle Abt, VP Card Marketing, Chase Manhattan Bank

"I think that the companies are trying to profit from the irresponsibility of young people."—Karia Velasquez, Senior, South Gate High School, Los Angeles, age 17

"Adults can't even handle money. How can minors handle it?"—Miguel Flores, Senior, Roosevelt High School, Los Angeles, age, 16

"What issuers discovered is that if you get your hooks into a consumer early, there's a loyalty that springs from that."—Bob McKinley, Analyst, Ram Research Corporation

"One out of every five U.S. teens has access to credit cards, according to a study conducted by Dennis Tootelian, professor of marketing at California State University. More than half of the students interviewed, the study showed, spend up to five hours a weekend shopping, mostly for clothing and accessories."—*National Enquirer,* April 14, 1992

"Roper College-Track, a research company that studies the college population, says that 51 percent of college students have a credit card. They frequently, according to the studies, have no idea how interest accrues on credit cards or how much debt they're accumulating compared to what they stand to earn when they graduate."—Alina Matas, *Miami Herald*, June 5, 1994

"One danger of credit for college-age people is that it makes them feel like adults, perhaps before they're ready. They may feel that they're entitled to own expensive things before they've earned them."—Dr. Kenneth O. Doyle, Financial psychologist, University of Minnesota

"Banks don't offer credit cards just because they like you. They offer them because they make money when customers use credit cards.

"The interest rate on a credit card can be 18 percent or even higher. Credit is pretty expensive.

"If you're not careful when you use a credit card, you could find yourself in a lot of debt.

"Without a credit card, it is just about impossible to rent a car, make a hotel or airline reservation, or even get a membership at a video store."—From a sales brochure published by Young Americans Bank, soliciting teenagers for credit cards.

"What I hear a lot is, 'I can't afford it, so I put it on a credit card.'"—Dr. Kathleen Gurney, Financial psychologist, Cincinnati, Ohio

"You learn by doing things. We'll learn how to control our credit-card spending by having cards. It should be one of the things you learn in college."—An anonymous student at Harvard Business School, 1994

"Some people will probably scream that it's consumer exploiting, but it seems to me to be of benefit to lawyers and clients."—Geoffrey Hazard, Professor, Yale Law School—on lawyers now accepting credit for payment of legal bills

"Another favorable aspect of credit cards at our supermarkets is that the average transaction is $19, compared with $8.50 when the customer forks over cash." —Glen E. Eley, Assistant Controller Imperial Foodtown Stores, Dayton, Ohio, *Business Week*, November 9, 1974

"When banks were paying 15 percent for *their* money, an argument might have been made for them charging 20 percent interest on credit cards. However, when the discount rate falls four times in less than two years to its current level of 5 percent and credit card interest rates remain stubbornly stuck to the roof, something is obviously wrong."—Rep. Charles E. Schumer (D-N.Y.) before The Consumer Affairs Subcommittee of The House Bank Committee, October 9, 1991

"I had a client, a decorator. He was enormously successful in the eighties. He used his credit cards for everything, and he spent prodigiously. He went to Paris like we'd drive to the library. He entertained at the best restaurants and bought expensive gifts for his customers and friends. When the recession hit in the nineties, his business went belly-up. He owed $200,000 in credit-card bills and couldn't pay them. Some of the companies offered to settle for half and restore his cards which they'd cut off, but he couldn't come up with a dime. Finally, he went into bankruptcy. It was granted, and he got a notice from the court which said, 'You have been discharged from all your debts.'

"In the same mail, he got a 'pre-approved' letter from American Express. He filled it out, and three weeks later he got a gold card. Now, he's back in debt. He can't file bankruptcy for another seven years, but he filed Chapter Thirteen and is paying his new debts with disposable income over five years.

"Look, the card companies take calculated risks. They know they're going to lose out on a certain percentage of customers, but if they were too careful, the credit checking and processing would be too costly, and it would cut down their cardholders and volume. Most people pay their bills...but the $200,000 this guy owed isn't that unusual."—Jeffrey S. Shinbrot, Bankruptcy attorney, Beverly Hills, California

"People go bankrupt because a job has been lost, or a costly medical problem has arisen, or a marriage has broken up or—most common of all—they have overused their credit cards. Back in the forties you had—nationwide—ten thousand bankruptcies. At the current rate it won't be long before ten thousand cases are filed in Philadelphia bankruptcy court alone."—Mitchell Miller, Bankruptcy attorney, Philadelphia, Pennsylvania

"My credit cards saved my life. I had a job, a car, a nice apartment. Then, I lost my job. I ran through my savings, and I was literally broke. I lived on my cards for nearly two years. I'd borrow cash from one account to pay my bills or I'd charge them, then I'd draw out cash from another account to pay out on the first one. I think without them, I would've jumped off a bridge. They got me by until I finally got another job. When the cards expired, I framed them and hung them on my wall."
—Philip J. Robinson, Detroit, Michigan

"The card was not created or ever intended to encourage people to spend beyond their means."—Joe Titus, original credit manager, The Diners Club—in 1959

"Oceans of direct mail touting so-called pre-approved cards, cards for teens and college kids. Ever-higher credit limits. Merchandise giveaways, cash rebates, and sweepstakes tied to card usage. Glitzy TV spots selling high style, high living, and glamour. No doubt about it: in just a few short years, card marketing has caught a good case of Proctor and Gamble."—John Stewart, *Credit Card Management* magazine, November, 1989

"The increasing default rate [on credit cards] is certainly the result of the increased marketing by the credit underwriters. As this becomes a greater problem, more people will point the finger at the people who issue cards."—Rep. Charles E. Schumer, (D-N.Y.), November, 1989

"Hogwash! The reat majority of American consumers are intelligent, responsible people not easily led into debt problems by TV and direct mail."—Joanne Black, Senior Vice-President, MasterCard, November,1989

"I believe in paying cash for dinners when I go out. I don't want people thinking that it was business, even though it's business."—Steve Ross, The late Time-Warner CEO, in Connie Bruck's, *Master of the Game*—1994

"Some people will misuse the card. Some will get in a helluva lot of trouble because of it, but there are always people misusing 'money' and always people getting into trouble because of it. That's all the damn thing is. It's simpler, easier, more efficient money. In a way, we're their bankers, but we're not their keepers."—Ralph E. Schneider, Chairman, the Diners Club—in 1959

"George Orwell in his novel *1984*, predicted that a fictitious leader called 'Big Brother' would control the life of every man, woman, and child in the world.

"Orwell might very well have been writing about the 'checkless society.' For it's likely that the bankers who control the economy—and 'they who control the purse strings, control the power'—will therefore, be the real managers of the one-card world."—Martin J. Meyer, in his 1971 book, *Credit-cardsmanship*

"The state of California is a credit-card junkie—a credit-card junkie who can't get its act together and keeps using the plastic."—Kathleen Brown, State comptroller and candidate for governor, California, July, 1994.

NUMBER EIGHT
BEN—THE SHOPPER

Ben just shrugged and smiled when he was told that his Aunt Mildred had deposited ten thousand dollars in a savings account for him. "Actually," he thought, "I could do a lot with ten thousand dollars." When a few weeks later he received a MasterCard application from the same bank, an obvious result of the deposit, he smiled and shrugged again. He filled out the application, leaving some spaces blank like occupation and place of business—he was unemployed. Nevertheless, not too long after returning the application, he got a credit card with a three-thousand-dollar credit limit. He sat in front of his TV set and started ordering things from those home-shopping programs and charging them. In four days, he had reached his limit. When he got the invoice, he typed out a letter on his computer asking the bank to increase his limit, withdrew the required minimum payment from the savings account, and paid the bill.

Within a few months, he had charged six thousand dollars in TV merchandise, including stacks of compact discs, Ginsu knives, and home-exercise equipment. And a football signed by O. J. Simpson.

He decided not to pay his next credit-card bill.

A lady from the collection department at MasterCard called his home and asked for Ben.

"Oh, he's in school," said his mother.

"Oh," said the lady from MasterCard, "is he a college student?"

"College student?" said his mother. "He's only twelve."

Chapter Nineteen

THE DEBTORS

"MOST BANKRUPTCIES I review involve credit cards to one degree or another," says James Dumas, bankruptcy and debt attorney and a bankruptcy panel trustee for the central district of California. "About 20 percent of all bankruptcies I see involve *only* credit-card debt. They're divided into two basic groups. Group one are people who simply can't control their credit-card spending. These people start getting more and more cards, pyramiding them to pay the minimums. Often the interest they pay becomes equal to their disposable income. They never think that what they're doing is wrong. 'I was always current,' I'm often told. 'It just started getting out of hand a few months ago.'

"Category two are people who have made a conscious effort to use cards without paying the bills. 'America grants freedom of speech, the right to bear arms, and a right to use a credit card' is their attitude, and 'I have a right not to repay.'

"I've seen people with annual incomes of $20,000, with $150,000 in credit-card debt. Even more amazing is the law doesn't permit me to object to this systematic fraud. And the card issuers never show up at bankruptcy hearings to complain.

"The biggest credit-card debt I was ever involved with was $200,000. It was 120 percent of the cardholder's annual income.

"The credit-card companies seem to concentrate on keeping balances current. They don't appear to be concerned with the issuance of dozens of cards to one individual. You get the feeling that settling for a certain percentage of a nonpayers' debt is part of their marketing plan and that it doesn't matter if that percentage of bad debt is high as long as volume and cardholder lists keep growing.

"Would bankruptcies be hitting the record numbers we're seeing these past years if credit cards had never been invented or had never reached their current popularity? No.

"The incredible thing is that many of the people who go into bankruptcy because of credit-card debt try to hide at least one or two of their cards. They don't want to surrender them, despite the problems the cards have caused.

"We're a society with an aging population that's spending, not saving. Two-thirds of the economy is consumption, and an increasingly large part of the problem are credit cards."

Ann Sullivan, a marketing manager in the Washington area owed $11,875 on six credit cards early in 1994. If she charged no more and only made minimum payments, it would, according to the consumer group Bankcard Holders of America, take twenty-seven years to pay the debt. In that period, she would have paid interest of $10, 621, bringing her total payment to $22,496. Bankcard Holders says that almost half of those using revolving credit-card plans make only minimum payments, typically 2.5 percent of the balance.

Under the tutelage of Bankcard Holders counselors, Sullivan switched to lower-interest cards which absorbed most of her debt, raised her payments, and worked out a plan to repay her debt in three years. Her interest will be $2,462 which will make the total payment $14,337, a savings of $8,159.

◆　◆　◆

"We have a lot of people taking on a lot of credit who don't know how to handle it," says Charlene Sullivan, associate professor of finance at Purdue University Business School.

◆　◆　◆

Over a period of eighteen months, Peter Ward of Manchester, Connecticut, secretly amassed twenty-five cards, many in his wife's name without her knowledge, according to a 1991 story in the *Wall Street Journal*. Then, he went on a buying spree. His purchases included trips for the family, pricey clothing, new furniture, a new refrigerator, a new sun deck, and a fence around their home. He flew relatives in for visits, first class.

"It was self-esteem," says Mr. Ward. "I figured if I had all these credit cards then I must be somebody."

His wife had no idea they were going into debt. She assumed business was great. By the summer of 1989, Ward was drawing cash on some credit cards to meet the minimum payments on others. Then, in December of that year, he broke his leg. His wife started to open the mail. What she opened mostly were credit-card bills.

In his desk, she discovered a folder full of monthly statements. She computed them. They came to thirty-five thousand dollars. Their combined income at the time was sixty thousand dollars.

After months of negotiating with card companies and near bankruptcy, they started to pay off their debts. They went from high living to total austerity and sixty-hour workweeks. The cards were gone. In a year they had repaid five thousand dollars. They've cashed in their I.R.A. account and have no savings, but they keep paying. "Someday I'll have beautiful things," says Mrs. Ward. "But for now, I just want to pay my bills."

◆   ◆   ◆

"It's the instant gratification ethic that prevailed in the 1980s," says Jay Muzychenko, of the National Foundation for Consumer Credit. "And it hasn't gone away."

◆   ◆   ◆

*Sarah Cole has a reoccurring nightmare in which she's being chased by large black dogs. She doesn't need a psychiatrist to explain that the dogs represent the bill collectors who phone her nearly every night and have, of late, even started to leave messages for her at the school at which she teaches. Her income is thirty-two thousand dollars a year. Her credit-card debts now total thirty-five thousand dollars. She's paying some of these debts at one thousand dollars a month—about 38 percent of her paycheck *before* taxes—and they still call because she doesn't have enough money to pay off all of her creditors.

"The money I owe is always on my mind." Sarah says, "even in my dreams."

◆　◆　◆

"You've got to go back generations to find people with a firsthand awareness of hard times," points out Luther R. Catling, president of New York's Budget and Credit Counseling Services. "The average twenty-five or thirty year old was raised by parents who also grew up in a healthy economy. These new debtors just didn't plan for money troubles they'd never experienced in the past."

◆　◆　◆

Craig Stock, a *Philadelphia Inquirer* financial columnist, wrote of a young woman he calls *Marcy. From the time she was eighteen, Marcy collected credit cards and went on shopping binges. "My first card had a three-thousand-dollar limit," she told him. "I thought, three thousand dollars, wow! Everybody's going to have a great Christmas. I hit the limit the first night I had the card, just before Christmas. It took me three hours."

The stress of owing so much gives her headaches and a constant pain in her stomach—actually, a tense, clutching feeling.

"I just feel like I have nothing to show for it," she told Stock. "Some furniture. Big deal."

For six years, Marcy got loans from banks and from her company's credit union to pay her credit-card bills. The pains and the anxiety continued, and so did her spending. She cut up the cards then got new ones.

Now, six years after getting her first card, and up to her neck in loans to pay for them, she still owes twenty-eight thousand dollars. Her annual salary, before taxes, is twenty-one thousand dollars.

◆   ◆   ◆

Joseph Merando was a forty-thousand-dollars-a-year sales manager for a new-home developer in the late eighties. He and his wife, Juanita, had two daughters and were conservative spenders. "I had great credit," Joseph told the *Ladies Home Journal* in 1991. "I was always able to pay my bills."

But Joseph's income was mostly from commissions and in October, 1988, their native Florida was hit by a real-estate slump. His earnings also slumped; then virtually disappeared, dropping to six thousand dollars that year. The Merandos began taking cash advances on their credit cards to meet their mortgage payments and other expenses, and they started charging for groceries and, even, medical care. They reached the limits on their cards and were paying from 18 to 21 percent interest. They had nowhere to turn. They kept applying for and getting new cards.

By 1990, they were into the credit-card companies for twenty-two thousand and couldn't meet all the monthly minimum payments.

After months of being dunned, they worked out deals. They're both working now. They live on tight budgets and are repaying the money.

Juanita has developed an aversion to credit cards, even though the cards really got them through their tough times. She works at a bank now. Her job? To solicit credit-card applications.

◆　　◆　　◆

Michael and Cynthia Proctor never requested their first credit cards. Pitches and applications for four of them were their mailbox in a one-week period. This was in 1982, and their combined income was under twenty-nine thousand dollars a year. They filled out the applications and got the cards and they liked them. By 1985, they liked them so much that they owned sixty-three of them. They also owed thirty-two thousand dollars and were at least six weeks behind on most payments.

They went into counseling, made a deal with the card companies, and got out of debt in six painful years, after flirting precariously with bankruptcy.

Their hobbies no longer include collecting credit cards.

◆   ◆   ◆

Elizabeth Hudson wrote of her life as a credit-card debtor in the July 14, 1986, issue of *Newsweek*. It was a familiar story of having a good job, enjoying a substantial increase in her standard of living, then leaving the job and trying to maintain that standard by using her MasterCard and Visa cards. "It was a grand arrangement," she wrote, "until I saw my debts mounting like those of a Third World country."

She related the story of her travails with the credit-card issuers, trying to work out something but getting lost in a world of red tape, confusion, and hardball. "One credit-card company taught me about bureaucracy," she related. "My letters (explaining my predicament) went unanswered. My phone calls were unresolved with responses like, 'We'll have to get back to you on that.'

"I received a form letter demanding payment or a reasonable explanation. I forwarded an account of my problem, only to receive the form letter again. Then the very same company sent me a 'special invitation' to apply for this card."

Pondering bankruptcy, she received still another offer of a card, "Dear Beth Hudson: We are offering this special card, with a credit line of five thousand dollars, to a very select group of people. People like you who handle credit very responsibly."

◆   ◆   ◆

Psychotherapist Yvonne Kaye remembers her own experiences with the addiction to "buying" which she compares with abuse of drugs, alcohol, and food. "Compulsive debtors," she says, "are people who can get a high from biochemical changes that occur when they spend money."

Kaye, a recovered debt addict herself, conducts therapy for debtors and has written a book, *Credit, Cash and Co-dependency: The Money Connection*. She remembers when she'd go through catalogs at 3:00 a.m. and order $1,000 items or when she'd spend $225 on groceries just for herself and her son. "Just as alcoholics must avoid alcohol," she says now, "compulsive spenders must avoid unsecured debt like personal loans and credit cards."

◆　　◆　　◆

Getting into trouble because of compulsive spending isn't restricted to people who are just getting by or who are not just getting by. People with lots of money can have financial problems because they can't control their spending, too. They just have more to spend, and it takes longer. Then suddenly they don't have lots of money anymore.

In 1992, Jack Clark was one of the best-known home-run hitters in baseball. Even though his career was on the downside (it would totally expire by the end of the 1992 season), he was pulling down an annual salary of more than $3 million. He also had an outstanding American Express bill of $55,955, a Visa bill of $19,820, and owed $400,000 in back taxes. His debts were listed at $6.7 million when he filed for bankruptcy at year-end '92.

No one is suggesting that a credit-card company should think twice about giving a card to a guy making $3 million a year. Irresponsibility, very frequently, works both ways.

◆   ◆   ◆

Author Joseph C. Goulden tells his credit-card adventure story: "In 1968, as Washington correspondent for the *Philadelphia Inquirer*, I spent time at both national conventions and then on the road with Humphrey and Nixon.

"There is a tradition among political reporters that the guy nearest the door puts the dinner tabs on his credit card; everyone else tosses in cash. (The split is always equal: if there are five reporters present and you have a tomato sandwich, you still pay as much as the guy who had a steak, cheesecake, and nine martinis.)

"In any event, I was in the last stages of a failed marriage, and I'd taken up with a gal who was so fast she left skid marks. Giving her the attention she required meant making expenditures that I did not want on my credit card. I began grabbing cash at the reporters' dinner table and paying with plastic. So it went, for more than a month on the road. The cash, of course, financed my fun.

"Then the day of reckoning: in October I had enough of daily journalism after a decade, and I decided to quit and write books full time.

"Two days after leaving the *Inquirer* payroll, American Express caught up with me, with a bill for about fourteen hundred dollars—shade less than one tenth of the annual salary I had been drawing and a substantial chunk of what I had put aside to finance my start as a free-lancer. If I paid the fourteen hundred dollars from my nest egg, I would be hurting.

"I had noticed, somewhere, an ad wanting 'adult book' manuscripts, so I wrote off for a spec sheet. I went into my office and wrote two in five days, more or less nonstop. I mailed the first one, and a check for $750 was back to me—much faster than, say *Harper's* or *The Nation*. I waited a week and sent off the second. Another $750, pronto. I breathed a sigh of relief and lived happily ever after, and I've now published eighteen books, not counting those quickies.

"In recognition of why I was doing the books, I included a scene where a guy used an American Express card to tickle the clitoris of a housewife neighbor he was trying to seduce. This turned out to be the only change the editor made in my manuscript: he deleted the words 'American Express' and let the deed be done only by a 'credit card.'"

◆　　◆　　◆

In a 1988 story in *People* magazine, Jean Reilly, of Phoenix, talked about getting two bank cards in 1980 when her annual income was twelve thousand dollars. She soon was into charging so enthusiastically that within a few years she had twenty-eight credit cards, including five Visas, two MasterCards, and an American Express. The rest were merchant cards.

By 1984, she had spent years moving charges and payments from one card to another, primarily by drawing cash to pay her minimum balances. She still owed twenty-two thousand dollars.

She sought help and got it from her local Consumer Credit Counseling Service. She quit cold turkey, going through withdrawal pains not dissimilar to many other addictions and, in the course, "fell off the wagon" at times. But she persevered. Now, like any other kind of reformed addict, she won't even touch a credit card.

Getting addicted to credit cards doesn't carry the stigma of other addictions. There are no hangovers, but there can be ulcers or nervous breakdowns or other ailments caused by the anxiety of owing a lot of money.

Are these stories unusual? Yes, in the sense that they are the exception and not the rule. But they are a weighty exception and they have a profound influence on debt in this country.

The Philadelphia law firm of Becket and Watkins specializes in bankruptcies. They have a staff of 155, including 22 lawyers. In 1993, they handled twenty-five million dollars in credit-card bankruptcies, and Pennsylvania is small potatoes compared to California, the bankruptcy capital of the world. There more than 100,00 such petitions are filed each year.

James T. Watkins, of the Becket and Watkins firm, says that about 40 percent of all bankruptcies his firm is involved with "result from charge-card spending."

The National Foundation for Consumer Credit Counseling says a typical client who comes to them with problems caused by misuse of their credit cards makes about twenty-four thousand dollars a year, owes about twenty-two thousand dollars, and has an average of ten credit cards.

Bankruptcy attorney Elizabeth Swank of Laguna Hills, California, says the average number of cards held by her clients is between fifteen and twenty. "The balances on these cards have ballooned as well," she says. "Four or five years age, the average credit-card debt for someone filing for bankruptcy was about twelve thousand dollars. Today it's more than twenty thousand dollars."

In 1972, Belinda of Los Angeles was nineteen years old, making two hundred dollars a week and carrying nine credit cards including a MasterCard and a Visa card. For the next twenty years, she was a compulsive shopper almost always financed by her credit cards. She would reach her limit on one card then get another to finance the minimum balances on the others she held. For three years in the eighties, she paid for a coke habit with cash advances from her cards. She knocked around various jobs, once pulling down forty-five thousand dollars a year as an advertising art director, but she never stayed long in one job. To calm her nerves, she became a compulsive eater, and she gained forty pounds.

By 1992, she was thirty thousand dollars in debt and was still paying for her shopping and eating with her credit cards and for her credit-card bills with other credit cards. She now had a Visa Gold and an Amex Gold and an Amex Optima, among other accounts.

That year she joined Debtor's Anonymous, the nationwide organization run much like Alcoholics Anonymous and Gambler's Anonymous. You go to meetings, tell your story, and toe the line. You abstain—in this case from credit-card use—or you are kicked out.

It worked. One night Belinda took a carving knife and sliced her credit cards up into tiny pieces.

There are days when she thinks, "Wouldn't it be nice to go out and buy some new clothes—maybe even open a charge account at the May Company or get a Visa card?" She entertains those thoughts for about five minutes, then, "I let it go. I know what that leads to for me."

◆   ◆   ◆

A fellow I know who we shall call *Mark says, "Credit cards are the greatest invention since the wheel. I have lived for twenty years on credit cards. When things were very good, I lived high and paid my bills. When times were tough, I paid minimums and occasionally was delinquent. Sometimes they took away some of my cards, but I always got new ones and I always paid up.

"I don't know what I would have done without them. I've been tapped out on loans from my family and friends, and no bank would loan me a dime, but they've done OK with me because I've never run out on a debt, and I've paid some pretty serious interest.

"There were times when the only way I could get a meal or a bed to sleep in was because I had a credit card. Who knows? I may have shot myself or jumped off a bridge if I didn't have them. I once started a business just with credit cards. It was successful and I lived good for five years off it. When it finally went under, the only thing I had left was my company credit card. I still have it. I couldn't live without it."

NUMBER NINE

Case History

BYRON, THE SWINGING BANKER

Byron Moger was a study in contradictions. He was a banker who didn't respect money. A vice-president at Manufacturer's Trust in New York, he became much like a drug dealer who "uses" as well as sells. He was enamored of credit cards. He was also much enamored of women and high times. An up-and-coming executive in Manufacturer's chain of command, he went through a string of failed marriages and unpaid debts before moving to Europe to escape his creditors. There, credit cards enabled him to buy beautiful jewelry for beautiful women and to get big cash advances at British casinos which he promptly reinvested and lost at their gaming tables.

Deep in debt in England, he returned to America and borrowed money from friends—money he never repaid. Now the credit-card companies, which along with the loans had been financing his various escapades, started canceling his accounts.

A few weeks before Christmas, he flew to Los Angeles, and flashing his one-remaining credit card, a Beverly Hills Hotel account, he checked into that celebrated inn.

By the end of the month, he took stock of his situation. He was flat broke. He'd run out of both credit and friends who would lend him money. An insurance policy on his life, on which his sons were beneficiaries, would run out on January 1 without payment.

The hotel was demanding he pay his bills, or else.

Byron ordered one last elegant room-service meal with champagne, finished both, and killed himself. He left the one-remaining credit card on the table and a hefty tip for the waiter.

Chapter Twenty

"BEATING THE SYSTEM"

IN A 1989 ARTICLE in the *Utne Reader*, a man named Gary Richardson gloated that he hadn't had a full-time job in four years and that, "I live on credit cards and (almost) nothing else." He reported that he had fifteen MasterCards, twenty-one Visas, three Discovers, and various others, that at the time he had $137,550 in unsecured revolving-credit accounts. He lives well, he said, "better than most people who work.

"As long as I keep paying my credit accounts every month and then borrowing the money back—and as long as my credit limits keep getting raised to meet my needs—I do well.

"I suppose," he continued, "this is a crime. But I don't care."

In conclusion, he wrote, "To me, whoever owes the most money wins. I intend to die a winner."

In 1993, bank-card issuers around the world charged off $1.78 billion to fraud. Unless the introduction of cards with the user's photos on them and the refine-

ment of electronic communications between the merchant and the credit-card companies at point of sale
proliferate at a much greater rate than now, it is expected that the years from 1994 to 2000 will not see a huge
percentage decline in the fraudulent use of credit and
debit cards.

There will be an increase in actual dollars lost
because charge volume will increase sharply.
Assuming, conservatively, that bank cardholders will
charge in excess of $10 trillion in that seven-year span,
fraud losses will exceed $14 billion. The problem is
that, as in the case of money, there are people sitting up
nights figuring out how to beat the system and make a
killing. New scams are being concocted every day.

Photos and fingerprints will not circumvent the
crook, for example, who has refined the art of applying
for credit cards by using social-security numbers and
other information "borrowed," or pilfered, from unsuspecting dupes, usually people they don't know.

Eventually, the much-anticipated "smart card," with
its "magic" microchip, will carry a PIN (personal identification number) and will have a marked impact on
fraud, but crooks keep on coming up with angles.

William Atherton, a Southern California private
investigator who specializes in bankruptcy cases for
Visa and MasterCard, has stories of people with so
much chutzpah that one's head reels.

One such case involved a crook who applied for and
received credit cards using a total stranger's name, bank
records, and social-security number. For twenty years,
he paid the bills, finally pyramiding charges until he
was fifty thousand dollars in debt and couldn't get any

more credit. He then did what any red-blooded American citizen would do, he filed for bankruptcy—under the other guy's name; a man he had never met but with whose credentials he had been living for two decades. And—he actually showed up at the bankruptcy proceedings, identifying himself as his victim and producing faked identification. One would think he'd be languishing in jail, but he's not. The case is still pending.

Atherton remembers a woman named Julie Marie Jolley of Los Angeles who, for several years, lived off credit cards she'd applied for and received using other people's names, social-security numbers, and other credit information. Two hundred thousand dollars in debt, she, too, preceded to file bankruptcy under the names of the people she had used. Unlike the fellow above, she's serving a twenty-one-month prison term.

"Sometimes," says Bill Atherton, "crooks just make up social-security numbers and even bank information. Sometimes it's caught and sometimes it's not. Usually, they just use other people's."

A guy named Kenneth Ayob tops Atherton's all-time credit-card fraud list. Using different names, he filed four bankruptcies involving an estimated $500,000, none under his actual identity.

"My first case was back east," Atherton recalls. "It involved a guy who had been convicted of bank fraud and was out on probation and repaying the money he'd stolen.

"He then applied for six credit cards in his father-in-law's name and ran up $100,000 in charges. Then he filed for bankruptcy under his own name. He listed the

hundred grand his father-in-law owed and the money
he still owed the bank for the fraud conviction as his
principal debts. He actually got away with the bankruptcy, but they revoked the earlier probation and he
was returned to jail. His father-in-law assaulted and
almost killed him in the courtroom."

According to Atherton, Visa and MasterCard have
started to actively encourage banks to appear at credit-
card bankruptcy cases, fraudulent or otherwise. When I
pointed out that a number of bankruptcy lawyers had
told me that they've never encountered bank representatives at such hearings, he shrugged. "They're big companies," he said, "and they're very busy. Eventually,
they'll have people at all of these things."

This type of fraud is just part of the criminal pattern.
Stolen cards, counterfeiting, and predominantly, theft
of cards that are then used by the thieves until the loss
is reported abound. Visa, MasterCard, Diners Club,
American Express—all have security forces around the
world.

Holograms have cut down on counterfeiting which,
in the early years of the credit card, caused the major
losses from fraud. Credit-card crime now brings down
not only "the card cops" but the T-men.

"Let's face it," my friend Joe Tilem says, "if you
counterfeit credit cards, you're counterfeiting money."

Just before Christmas in 1992, the Palm Beach,
Florida, sheriff's office arrested two Asian males in their
hotel room. They discovered fourteen counterfeit cards
and a list of eight additional card account numbers.

The arrest had come about because of a tip that a

gang of illegal aliens was operating a counterfeit credit-card ring in the area. More arrests followed in Palm Beach. Then, in late January, a U.S. Secret Service agent in Miami, reacting to a call from a suspicious department-store security director, followed four Asian males as they toured a Sak's Fifth Avenue situated in a mall. The agent watched them purchase a wide variety of expensive merchandise, using various credit cards, then called for help, and the men were detained. In their car, police found more cards and eighty-five credit-card account numbers later determined to have already been used in more than $400,000 worth of fraudulent transactions.

The next day, Secret Service agents searching the suspects' hotel rooms found 139 embossed counterfeit credit cards, 87 unembossed cards, an internal bank printout containing more than 200 account numbers, and various fake driver's licenses and other counterfeit identification. It was clear that they were members of the same group as the men arrested in Palm Beach.

The gang was traced to Los Angeles where eight more members were arrested. Eventually, it was discovered that the roots of the operation were in Hong Kong where local authorities, working with the Secret Service, collared the remaining members.

It was estimated, based on the cards and card numbers recovered and their potential buying power, that the arrests saved the industry an estimated $17 million.

The case, while under investigation, was given the code name, Operation Plastic Dragon.

◆   ◆   ◆

A plant in Marlborough, Massachusetts, that manufactured Visa and MasterCards went bankrupt in 1980, and everything on the premises was auctioned off. One enterprising entrepreneur bought more than a million bank credit cards for a hundred dollars. He immediately called Visa and MasterCard, notified them that he had the cards and wanted one dollar for each of them—a ransom of something like $1.2 million.

He added that if they didn't agree to his offer, he would release them on the black market. That threat was his mistake.

The credit-card companies negotiated with him, worked him down to accepting $200,000, met with him at his office, handed him the money, and promptly had him arrested for extortion. He served two years in jail. The cards were destroyed.

Almost from the inception of the all-purpose credit card, there were many thieves.

As early as 1951, a break-in at the company which printed the early Diners Club cardboard credit cards, saw a gang of robbers make off with more than a thousand cards. This was before the cards were usable at stores or for airline tickets or other resalable merchandise or services. After a few hundred dollars in restaurant charges, the thieves were picked up at the Oyster Bar in Grand Central Station because a suspicious restaurant manager doubted that the ill-dressed surly characters who presented Diners cards to pay for their dinners matched the profile of club members. A call to the Diners Club offices verified that no such numbers and names existed. The manager called the police who arrested the now well-fed perpetrators.

A Diners Club executive, the late Phil Adelman, looked up from his dinner at New York's glossy Little Club one night and saw, across the room, one of the young men who worked in the Diners Club mailroom sitting with a girl and lapping up champagne and sirloin. Adelman, who headed the Diners Club legal department, waited until the man handed the waiter a credit card, then walked over to the cashier, and asked to look at it. It was a card that had been stolen from the company's offices where returned cards often sat around on the desks of people in the credit department. The mailroom clerk was fired with no charges pressed because of his youth. He had used the card only that one time. After that, security was tightened.

A 1961 article by McLeod Wylie, which first appeared in *Today's Living* and was then reprinted in *The Reader's Digest*, told the story of David Goldmeyer who, at the time, was considered "The nation's top credit-card thief" by the FBI. His "career" took him throughout the United States and to Mexico and Cuba. His modus operandi was to loot locker rooms at smart country clubs. He'd take cash and other valuables, but his specialty was credit cards. He'd rent cars, purchase jewelry, and even cash checks using the stolen cards as identification.

When captured, he admitted he had a quota of stealing or "charging" at least one thousand dollars a day, and if he missed that quota, he wasn't able to sleep.

Raymond Freudberg, chairman of the United National Group of Insurance Companies in Philadelphia, had lunch at a kosher Chinese restaurant on a Friday afternoon. Days passed before he realized he'd never gotten his card back. He notified the issuers of the MasterCard he'd paid the tab with. He was told that the card had been used immediately preceding the Friday night Jewish Sabbath, that it had not been used during the Sabbath hours and that it was used again that Saturday night and Sunday, immediately after the Sabbath. Quite obviously the card had fallen into the hands of a thief who might not have feared contemporary law but studiously respected biblical injunction.

The most remarkable credit-card crime and apprehension on record took place in the late sixties when a pickpocket named Ted Warren (among other names he used) lifted someone's wallet at a crowded St. Louis baseball game. Two days later, he showed up at a store, purchased various items of clothing, and presented the card. The woman who took it looked at it for quite a long time then excused herself. Warren was understandably nervous but remained calm. At least he did until the woman returned with a uniformed policeman who promptly arrested him. By the most amazing coincidence the police and, for that matter, anyone in any of the credit-card security departments, had ever heard, the woman was actually the wife of the man whose wallet had been lifted. The odds against such a happening are almost incalculable.

From the introduction of mail-order buying with credit cards, we were apprehensive about illegal use and, in the early years of the Diners Club, required mail-order companies to check each order with our credit department which would approve the charge. When the volume of such buying grew, we discontinued the practice and took losses.

No one who owns or rents a mailbox has not "won" a sweepstakes. My own current string of "you've almost made it" notes from Publisher's Clearing House has now continued for more than two years along with dozens of entreaties to subscribe to a magazine—any magazine—so that these notices might continue. I have, in each case, dutifully returned the enclosed card and envelope without subscribing to anything. I do it because I'm curious as to how long this relationship can continue without money being exchanged. They are apparently a cheap date. Should I win ten million or so, I will, however, out of gratitude, subscribe to every publication on the PCH list.

I have no doubts, incidentally, that eventually people do win the Publisher's Clearing House Sweepstakes. I am not quite as sure about others.

I've received, as have you, I'm sure, correspondence telling me I've won assorted Cadillacs, Caribbean vacations, luggage, and bundles of money. All I need do is buy something and then have my number picked from a hat or a jar or a bucket.

None of these particularly intrigued me. There was always, somewhere in the fine print the size of a gnat's tail, some revelation that although I had indeed become a "winner," I wouldn't actually get anything until I *really* won.

But an official-looking document, looking very much like a stock certificate, I fished out of my mailbox recently really fascinated me.

It declared that I had completed the first two stages of the All-American Sweepstakes and that I was ABSOLUTELY GUARANTEED (in capital letters) *at least one* of these four fabulous awards:

- brand-new Chrysler LeBaron, or $10,000 in cash
- two round-trip airfares to the Bahamas
- Sony thirty-two inch screen TV, or $1500 in cash
- $1,200 in cash

Since I had no recollection of having participated in the first two stages of this sweepstakes that I had been told I had successfully completed, I was amused.

I telephoned the 800 number listed on the certificate. A gentleman with a strong southern accent answered and proceeded to read all the information I had in front of me. He then congratulated me and told me he'd like to turn me over to his supervisor. First, could he have the expiration date on my credit card?

This was really getting interesting. I gave him the date, and he switched me to his supervisor who greeted me warmly and again congratulated me profusely, adding that I would soon receive a supply of beauty products and a Nashika camera, for it seems, a Japanese company named Nashika was the sponsor of the All-American Sweepstakes.

"Fine," I said.

After going on at length about the value of the beauty supplies and the camera and, once again, assuring me that I had won any one of the prizes which had now been reviewed for me three times, I was told that there would be a charge of $650, far less than the accumulated value of all the gifts I would receive, for what was described as shipping, handling, and processing. One assumes they were going to gift wrap my Chrysler LeBaron and ship it by air.

"Could I have the number of your credit card?" he asked casually.

"Well," I said, "send me the car first, and then I'll give you my credit-card number."

"If you're unhappy with your prize and the camera and the beauty supplies," he assured me, "you get your money back."

Sensing that I'm not physically or apparel-wise equipped for a cold day in hell, I demurred. The dialogue was ended.

The gimmick here, I am told, is that in games like this, you do get a prize—certainly one worth considerably less than your $650.

Well, maybe despite my skepticism, the All-American Sweepstakes is as straight as an arrow. I suspect not, but I am bothered most by the fact that credit-card issuers have an agreement with this type of operation and for example, with some of the absurdly inept products advertised on television; products such as exercise machines which have been researched and dismissed as worthless by legions of experts. People tend to succumb to sales pitches because buying simply by giving a credit-card number is so easy and because the presence of names like Visa suggest validity.

The cardholders who buy junk from radio, magazine, or newspaper advertisements, merely by sending along their card number, spend tens of millions of dollars a year. Who's checking the stuff out? Did someone at Visa or MasterCard really look into the Nashika All-American Sweepstakes or the common bedspring which was sold as a muscle builder on television before allowing them to use the card as a tool to solicit and, we assume collect, money with high-pressured mail and phone pitches?

It is a nagging suspicion I have that *anyone* who sells virtually *anything* can have access to Visa or Master-Card or American Express charge systems and that such access allows sales of dubious products and services to be made even more readily.

The card-issuer's responsibility should lie not only in deciding who uses the card but that what it is used for is reasonable and authentic. Scams, it seems, can work both ways. Granting a merchant the right to offer the faculties of a credit card infers an endorsement, and protection should be expected by the cardholder.

Of course, being shady seems to be a studied preoc-cupation that reached great heights in popularity when Charles Keating and others of his ilk became folk leg-ends in the eighties.

Being downright crooked is as old as mankind and requires almost as much ingenuity as being only shady, or somewhat pregnant.

Take the two men from Queens, New York, Michael Tannauzzo and Robert Santura, arrested in 1993 for being part of a ring that would steal credit cards, charge for merchandise up to the limits on the cards, and then, through the use of a stolen embossing machine, change the numbers on the cards to others they bought from employees or business owners of establishments that honored the cards. The ring they had been operating was netting its enterprising proprietors two million dollars a year.

Abusing a credit card knows no social or economic barriers. Anyone can play. Consider Rudolph L. Mazzei, a judge in Suffolk County, New York, who was barred from the bench for life because he forged his mother's name on a Visa gold credit-card application in 1989 to obtain money with which to gamble. The application was approved, and a card in his mother's name was issued. It wasn't until he'd run up some substantial charges, mostly from cash withdrawals, that the card issuer discovered the judge's mother had died years before he'd applied and that he had no plan to pay her bills.

The scams and thievery go on, destined to be slowed or halted eventually by the aforementioned personal identification numbers, fingerprint and signature cards, and other systems that could make credit-card crime something of a rarity. But even at this stage, when stolen-card markets and counterfeiting exist on a wide scale, credit-card crime is pretty much white-collar stuff. Unlike cash and other untraceable valuables, many holdup men often won't even bother to take a victim's credit card. Some have kept the wallet itself and discarded the cards which, once the crime is committed, involve additional risk.

Crime experts I interviewed said violence rarely accompanies credit-card theft, and more than a dozen criminologists I spoke to agreed that a cashless society in which people used a foolproof credit card to pay for everything would have a monumental effect on violent crime. The total use of credit-card charges—traceable money—would, of course, devastate drug traffic and black-market crime.

A cashless society would also have an interesting effect on the legitimate payment of taxes. No one has been able to accurately calculate either the enormous amount of income undeclared on tax forms because it is untraceable or the number of people who don't pay taxes at all for the same reason. I remember in the early 1950s, sitting in a New York nightclub with the owner, a notorious gangster named Frankie Dio, who was bemoaning the growing popularity of Diners Club cards. "It usta be," he growled, "I'd open up the register and take out cash, and no one knew the difference. Now, I go to the register, and it's fulla goddamn credit-card charges."

Progress, it seems, doesn't please everybody.

Case History	**NUMBER TEN** JOHN—THE RELUCTANT THIEF

*John Boland found a wallet in a public garage one day. It was lying there on the ground right between his car—a ten-year-old Chevrolet—and a dark green Jaguar convertible. The wallet, like the other car, was shiny and new. He stood and stared at it a long time before he bent over and picked it up. In it were two twenties and four one-hundred-dollar bills. The hundreds had obviously just been withdrawn from a bank because they were crisp and unwrinkled. He counted them, then counted them again. Then he returned them to the billfold. In the pockets of the billfold were various cards: a driver's license, an AAA membership, a social-security card, a Blue Cross ID, some memberships in health clubs and for a video store—and American Express, MasterCard, and Visa credit cards.

He looked at them longingly, then, after making sure no one was watching him, got in his car, and drove away.

Things had been rough for John. He'd lost his job at a Phoenix hotel a month before. He was in that particular garage because he'd applied for a job with another hotel chain. They'd taken his application and told him he'd hear from them if anything opened up; the same story he'd been hearing for a month.

He was running out of money. He had no family to support, but he'd never made much money and certainly never saved any. On this particular day, he had $26 in his pocket and $268 in a dwindling checking account. He had no idea how he was going to pay next month's rent. He couldn't apply for unemployment insurance because he held his last job for only a couple of months, and he'd used up his unemployment insurance before getting it.

As he drove away, he took the wallet from his pocket, set it up on the dashboard in front of him, and gazed at the cards and the cash in it.

As a desk clerk at hotels, he'd often come across credit cards left by guests. Once he'd even opened a briefcase a housekeeper had given him that had been left in a room by someone who had departed the hotel in a hurry. It contained various papers and books and an open envelope with nearly twenty thousand dollars in it. He imagined that some drug dealer, perhaps on the lam from the cops, had skipped town in a hurry.

John thought carefully about taking the money and returning the case and the rest of the contents. Who could say he took the money even if the owner did return? But he was too nervous to do it, so he turned the case over to the manager intact. A couple of hours later, the owner returned for the case he'd forgotten. The first thing he did was count the money, then he peeled off a twenty for the housekeeper and a twenty for John and left.

But, "This time," John thought, "this time it's untraceable."

When he arrived at this apartment, he took the cash and stuck it into his pocket. Then he transferred the driver's license, social-security card, and credit cards into his wallet.

"If I'm going to do this," he said to himself, "I've got to do it right away before this guy reports the cards missing."

He spent the rest of the day buying things. He bought clothes and luggage and a ring and a watch. Then he had lunch at a fine restaurant and, afterward, bought another watch, then another. Later in the afternoon, he took the watches to a dealer and sold all three for three thousand dollars. He kept rotating use of the credit cards.

That night he sat and tried to decide what to do next. By now, the owner of the cards would certainly have reported their loss. Could he risk using them again? He was up all night pondering the decision.

By the morning, he was a wreck. He'd never stolen anything before—well, maybe he'd shoplifted an occasional small item in a drugstore, and once he had been given a ten-dollar bill instead of a one for change in a supermarket, and he hadn't said anything, but that was not larceny. This was. He'd charged more than ten thousand dollars on three cards, and he'd go to jail if they ever caught him.

John went to the dining room of a nearby hotel and charged a big breakfast on one of his cards, but he couldn't eat. He signed for his meal and left. As he strolled through the lobby, he passed an airline counter. He decided to go for it. He bought a ticket for New York, in the name of the man whose wallet he had, then charged for it with his Visa card. He held his breath as they ran the card through the monitor.

As he walked away from the counter, his heart was beating so loudly that he could hardly think. Obviously, the owner of the wallet had not yet reported the loss, or the credit-card company was late in posting an alert on their computers.

He arrived in New York with his new luggage stuffed with his new clothes and his pockets bulging with cash. The only wallet he carried was the one he found. He was assuming the other man's identity. He took a cab to the Holiday Inn in midtown Manhattan. When he checked in, he decided to press his luck.

It was his first time in New York, and he loved it. He took long walks up and down Broadway and Fifth Avenue. He dined at good restaurants, and they accepted his card. Then, on the second day, he picked out a sports jacket at a clothing store on East Fifty-seventh Street. He handed the salesman a credit card and, as always, waited apprehensively. This time his fears were realized. The clerk returned looking troubled.

"I'm afraid," he said, "that there's a problem with your card."

John didn't want to hear another word. He turned and walked quickly out of the store. When he reached the street, he started a half trot, half fast-walk. He cut down Fifth Avenue and got lost in the midtown crowd. He didn't slow up until he was back in his room. Once there, he pulled out the credit cards and stared at them. The party's over, he decided. And he put them back in the wallet. He'd never use the cards again. But he still had a lot of cash, and he was in New York. He'd stay another couple of days, and then he'd head for home.

That night he had dinner at a good Italian restaurant just off Eighth Avenue. He paid cash. Then he went to a nearby bar and had a couple of drinks. He would keep at least two thousand dollars of the money he had, he decided. Then he'd return home, pay his rent, and look for a job. He would put the wallet in an envelope and return it with the cards to the guy who owned them. John would not, of course, include the cash.

He was putting his key into the lock of his hotel-room door when he heard someone crying. It was a woman, standing in the hall not ten feet from him.

"Are you OK?" he asked.

She looked up. Her handkerchief was pressed against one eye. "Are you a doctor?" Why on earth would she ask that? he wondered. He shook his head, "No, what's wrong?"

"I've got something in my eye," she murmured, her voice still quivering.

She moved close to him. She was young and pretty.

"Maybe I can help you," he suggested. He opened the door to his room, and they went in. He switched on the light, wet a hand towel, and moved it gently over her eye. After a minute or so of this, she slowly smiled.

"It's gone," she said softly. "How can I thank you?"

They made love all night. He ordered some fine imported wine, and they finished the bottle. Room service came up with dinner, then another bottle of wine. There was more sex.

When John woke up, his head was pounding and his stomach felt like he'd eaten the rug. The clock next to him read 1 p.m. The sun was streaming in through the blinds. He looked around the room. The girl was gone.

He stood up. It wasn't easy. Then it hit him what had happened. He flung open the closet. An empty hanger dangled, alone. The drawers were empty. She'd taken all his clothes. His watches—a new one and an old one—his cash and the wallet with all the credit cards.

She'd taken everything he had, packed them into the new luggage, and disappeared. He wrapped a sheet around his naked body and sat on the edge of the bed.

Fifteen minutes later, there was a knock on the door. He just sat. Then it opened and three men walked in. Two of them flashed badges.

When he arrived at the police station, he was wearing a towel and a raincoat one of the detectives loaned him. The third man who had entered the room was from the security force of one of the credit-card companies.

"Your girl friend," he explained to John, "tried to use your credit cards at Saks. But we were looking for it and they held her."

Now John got into the prisoner's garb they'd given him.

"The guy who lost the wallet was late in reporting it," the security man told him. "We would never have grabbed you if you'd stopped using it yesterday."

Chapter Twenty-One

WILL CASH DIE, AND OTHER OPINIONS, COMPLAINTS, AND PROGNOSTICATIONS

N. EUGENE LOCKHART, PRESIDENT AND CEO, MASTER-CARD: "By the year 2,000, 25 percent of all consumer purchases in the U.S. will be made by credit card. The rate of growth after that year will be determined by the speed in developing computer-chip technology.

"Growth will come from greater use in areas like supermarkets, insurance payments, and health benefits. In many cases, the industry will have to modify its rates charged to merchants. In some industries the margin is so thin, they can't accommodate a 2 percent service charge.

"The consumer used to feel that just using a charge card gave them something more than cash. Now, they look to added value—lower interest rates or fees, and premiums and rebates. Almost all the growth in the last three years has come from co-branded cards. People want airline miles or car or gasoline discounts—something extra. And the consumer will continue to demand more and more value.

"Have the card issuers made overspending easy? Sure, but cardholders and card companies are getting smarter all the time. They're learning how to use the cards and how to issue them. The industry is waking up to risk, More and more, they'll take public stances regarding the ethical problems of issuing credit cards.

"I have a sixteen year old in prep school. Every kid in his class has been solicited for a credit card.

"Card solicitation to college and high-school kids has to be studied. But, in the long run, the consumer has to make the choices. Like any good business people, banks are driven by growth. Smart ones realize, however, that everything's a balance. There's almost always a trade-off. If you give the cards to the wrong people, you'll suffer, too. Some have been very astute in playing the low-end market and learned how to issue cards to marginal risks who can and will pay their bills. Some have not."

ROBERT MCCRIE, PROFESSOR OF SECURITY MANAGE-MENT, JOHN JAY SCHOOL OF CRIMINAL JUSTICE: "I don't make predictions but certainly one would have to agree that there's a good chance cash will disappear.

"If it does, one would have to quickly agree that it is very likely that there would be a reduction in robbery and theft as a result of cash being replaced by some kind of computerized credit card, perhaps with a PIN number or some other kind of fail-safe protection.

"Drug sales, for example, would be affected strongly by a money system that could be tracked. The government is obviously constantly trying to figure out ways to make drug traffic more difficult. They discontinued the use of $500 and $1,000 bills so that the surreptitious movement of large sums of money would be made more difficult.

"It's always possible, of course, that another type of crime would be conceived if there was no cash, and it might rearrange some of it, but there's no question it would decrease crime as we know it today."

ROBERT ROSSEAU, PRESIDENT AND CEO, CITICORP, DINERS CLUB INCORPORATED: "I don't think cash will ever die. It's got portability that people need. If I get a hundred and want to give you fifty, I can do it readily with cash. It's more easily divisible. And it's backed by government, not just companies. But credit-card usage will grow enormously—someday there'll be a billion cards in the world.

"Yes, they will replace checks because it makes sense. Most banks don't like credit cards even if its their most profitable business. The Bank of America, for example, is the largest consumer bank in the country, but they're far from the top of the bank-card chart, and they don't seem to aggressively promote that business even though they were, more or less, the first big bank in the field.

"Where is the Diners Club going? To the businessman and the frequent traveler, high net-worth individual, the t-and-e people, whether what they charge is reimbursable or not. We cater to people who don't want to pay interest or penalty fees.

"We're not after a hundred million cards. I can see, perhaps, ten million U.S. off in the future.

"We'll flourish. Visa and MasterCard may not, at least not the way they exist today. Antitrust and price-fixing problems may cause the government to think about breaking them up and return many of their functions to the bank issuers.

"They're also going to have to think about the rates they're starting to charge to merchants and services. Some supermarkets are paying a fee of less than 1 percent. Their deal with the federal government to charge income taxes is being talked about at 1.6 percent. Can they live with those rates?"

ED HOGAN, SENIOR ADVISOR, MASTERCARD: "Credit cards are more accepted now than money. Try spending a drachma in the Bronx. The cards will continue to grow—even more so outside of the U.S.. The card will have processing abilities the mind hasn't even imagined yet. In fifteen years, you'll be able to order your airline tickets through your TV set. All TV will be credit-card ready. When you arrive at an airport, your smart card will have already picked your preferred seat and ordered your favorite meal.

"You'll be able to order your tickets to the theater or a concert or a ball park right on your TV screen, check out the available seats, and select the ones you want. You'll make purchases in a supermarket off unattended machines or kiosks in the market through your TV sets.

The card will pay for everything and accumulate discounts or rebates and charge everything. They'll even be keyed to order your favorite brands.

"Security will be absolute, and privacy will be guarded.

"A strong issuers's clearinghouse will cut down on card duplication and the practice of paying one credit card with another.

"When the problem gets big enough—it'll be solved."

JOHN STEWART, EDITOR AND PUBLISHER, CREDIT CARD MANAGEMENT MAGAZINE: "Were the card issuers careless in the issuing of credit cards? Yes. A lot of them simply didn't know what they were doing. But the recession in the late eighties and early nineties sent them a wake-up call. Credit losses soared, and they saw it on the bottom line. Look at American Express' Optima card. In 1987, Amex thought they had it made. They were used to people paying their bills, but most of their regular cardholders' bills were paid by companies. Individuals had to pay their Optima bills, and they ran up charge-offs of 10 percent.

"Well, everybody decided to come up with better ways to evaluate potential cardholders. Scoring models that evaluate applicants and establish charge limits have become so refined, they're capable of controlling spending to a much greater degree. Many of the problems they have today are coming from the poor judgment in issuing cards and establishing limits in the eighties.

"They're now even prescreening and scoring potential cardholders before they solicit them. They take a list, run it through a credit bureau, and kick out names that aren't potential users or could represent credit risks.

"It's happening. It's better. It's still not what it should be but it will be. The weapons are there. It's just a matter of getting everybody to use them.

"You can tell great stories about the people who misuse credit cards, but they're the exceptions and the figures are going down."

JORDON GOODMAN, WALL STREET CORRESPONDENT, MONEY MAGAZINE, AUTHOR OF EVERYONE'S MONEY BOOK: "Cash won't die, but it'll get very, very sick. I think that eventually credit cards will be used for 50 percent of all consumer buying. The smart cards will radically diminish the use of cash. People like to charge, and it's smart and convenient. I don't see a big future for debit cards in this country.

"Certainly, the ready availability of credit causes people to spend more than they can afford. Because of credit-card spending, retail sales are higher than they would have been without such cards. It gets a lot of people into trouble but has done more good than harm, and if 80 percent of all credit cardholders are paying their bills on time (as statistics indicate they are), that's a good record. It's especially good when one considers the recession and its aftermath.

"All the frills and add-ons that come with credit cards these days simply serve to distract from high-interest rates.

"Amex's new 'True Grace' card sounds good. The no-interest grace period is a good feature. They'll compete. They have to. They've gotten rid of their brokerages, also some other businesses not related to service, and now they can concentrate on coming up with new plans and marketing them, and they're good promoters."

ROBERT K. HAMMER, CHAIRMAN, INVESTMENT BANKERS, CREDIT-CARD CONSULTANTS: "Any prediction about the profitability of the bank credit-card industry over the next decade has to keep in mind that innovations are constantly increasing that potential. Certainly, the industry will move from branch banking to electronic banking to interactive banking with anybody with a PC or a television set being able to buy, sell, pay their bills, and keep their books at home or in their office on one unit. These innovations will, at first, actually tend to keep earnings and growth somewhat in check because of the costs of effecting them. I still see an 8 percent average growth in earnings through 2004. After that, in 2004, U.S. bank volume will be $750 billion and earnings, $17 billion. New techniques will curb fraud and counterfeiting.

"When it's finally in place on a large scale, interactive marketing and banking will dominate, and so will the bank card. Profits will be astronomical."

JEFF KUTLER, SENIOR EDITOR, THE AMERICAN BANKER: "Just a couple of years ago, researchers and many of us who cover the credit-card scene questioned whether it was a growth industry. That question is no longer asked. Growth rates may eventually decline somewhat. Some form of interactive home payments, possibly independent of credit-card plans, will compete. The younger generation likes interactive living through TV and computers, but credit cards simply make life too easy not to flourish. We won't see a checkless society in our lifetime, but it'll happen. The banks have made checks more efficient than ever. That will slow down their disappearance. But credit and debit cards are cheaper than checks for the banks and are simpler and require less effort for the consumer, so checks will go.

"Does that mean that the powers-that-be in banking have reached a consensus that they should move away from checks to a computer-based debit or credit-card system only? No. It hasn't happened.

"If we started all over again and had the technology we have now, we wouldn't have checks, but the banking industry hasn't asked itself that question. Why? The people who run the banks don't have efficiency and benefits to society on their front burners. Bankers are bankers because they traditionally take deposits and make loans.

"If the credit card wasn't so profitable, they wouldn't pay any attention to it. People who run banks tend to be from commercial, not consumer lending, and they make those profits on credit cards because they are making loans. It's really the same old function. They just don't treat it with the same respect. Others thoughts: I suspect that a lot of people, particularly younger people, will eventually trend away from revolving to debit credit.

"Co-branding has given the cards a big boost, but bankers are concerned that they're becoming bookkeepers for national brands, that they're becoming minor players.

"'Hey!' they're complaining, 'who's in charge here anyway?'"

CHUCK RUSSELL, FORMER PRESIDENT AND CEO, VISA, AND DIRECTOR, FIRST U.S.A. BANK, AND THE FIRST DATA CORPORATION: "Credit cards are part of the electronic data loop. That loop will be extended to include more point-of-sale terminals and automation. Cards will be accepted universally, just like money. They won't replace cash entirely but will make a huge dent in the use of checks. People are becoming more and more computer literate and more and more dependent on them. Visa did more to automate the world than any other service organization on earth in the last ten or fifteen years. We dragged the banks kicking and screaming into automation.

"Now, because of automation, brands like Visa and MasterCard will become meaningless, with more emphasis on the bank or other group providing the service, issuing the card, etc.

"Credit cards have saved major banks. Citibank was in deep trouble until they started emphasizing their card business, and so was Chase.

"Banks have not been remiss in the issuance of cards. Politicians love to make an issue out of it. They simply love to make speeches and pass bills. The worse credit-user in the United States is the government, and it's the people running the government who complain most about the banks being careless."

CHRISTOPHER WOOD, NEW YORK BUREAU CHIEF, THE ECONOMIST MAGAZINE: "Cash won't die. Credit cards will get more and more popular, but cash will always be around; if for no other reason than cash is confidential. It leaves no trail. Many people don't want a paper trail on their spending, and cash is clean and final. Some have a 'big brother' mentality. They don't want individuals at credit-card companies or banks checking out their spending habits, researching, and studying them. Some don't care; most don't think about it. Many do. There'll always be people who, for various reasons, want absolute privacy.

"Credit cards will never be as popular outside the U.S. as it is in it. In America cash is suspect. In other countries, cash is treated with respect. Sure, it would have an enormous effect on crime and secrecy. Maybe that's why it won't happen.

"The biggest danger to the card industry are the usurious interest rates. People get disgusted with paying those high interest rates. But it's mostly older people who are more suspicious of the cards and are wiser in using them. Younger people have grown up with them. They're simply part of their lives. And they use them with less care.

"If you think it's easy to get multiple cards and high credit limits here, you should check out the United Kingdom. Their computers don't even talk to each other."

NUMBER ELEVEN
ROY AND THE
PARK AVENUE APARTMENT

Living on Park Avenue, Roy had always thought, had to be the ultimate. "When I die," he told friends, "I want my obit to read 'Roy Green, of Park Avenue, died today.'"

When he was made vice-president of his company and was given a substantial raise, he was ready for the move. His wife, Sophia, wasn't all that sure. They'd lived on the Grand Concourse in the Bronx for the twelve years they'd been married. His parents had lived nearby in their tiny apartment since before he was born. But now, Roy was vice-president, and he was making more money than he had ever made in his life. The old man, now a widower, still persevered in his little tailor shop, just off the Concourse, pressing and cleaning and mending for the same people and their kids. He made what he described as "a nice living."

Within two months after getting his new job and raise, Roy and his wife were living in a Park Avenue apartment in the lower Seventies.

They emptied their savings account to furnish the place and went into their credit cards for another twenty grand for last-minute flourishes.

He was proud of his apartment. He started giving parties, and since they were on Park Avenue, they were elegant parties with waiters with white gloves and caviar and champagne and even chateaubriand which is actually steak with a great name and a great price tag.

Soon, even his increased salary couldn't handle Roy's swell new life, and he kept digging deeper into the credit-card companies.

One year after the move, he had nine different accounts and owed nearly seventy-five thousand dollars.

Roy and his wife would rent a limousine and once a month drive up to the Bronx to see his father. Once a month, the old man would take the subway down to Park Avenue. He'd walk around the beautiful apartment and sigh happily.

But high living got Roy and his wife on a spending kick that went beyond the apartment: designer clothes, Caribbean vacations, dinners at Manhattan's toniest restaurants. By the end of the second year in the apartment, they had sixteen credit cards and owed $165,000 on them, $15,000 more than his annual salary.

He started missing payments on his credit-card accounts, and a lien was put upon his salary. They took his cards away, and he was broke. The unthinkable happened. He couldn't pay the monthly rent on the apartment.

Roy was dejected and rode the subway to the Bronx. He told his father about his problems.

"How much is your rent?" the old man asked.

"Six thousand a month," Roy told him.

"You know," said the old man, "for three months I'd like to live on Park Avenue, too." And he wrote out a check for eighteen thousand dollars and moved to Park Avenue. Every day, he'd walk to the Seventy-second Street subway, and every night, he'd come home to Park Avenue. He'd stretch out on the living-room sofa, and Roy's wife would serve him dinner while he and Roy watched TV on the forty-eight-inch set in the room.

After three months, they all moved back to the Bronx.

Chapter Twenty-Two

WHAT

I THINK

WILL CASH REALLY DIE? Yes. Most likely a combination of credit cards and debit cards offering total charge availability and/or chits or scrip will become a way of life by the middle of the twenty-first century. There is no reason for it not to happen and every possible reason for it being.

At this writing, Kate, my youngest daughter, is four. There will come a time in her life when she will not use cash.

This will have an enormous impact on theft and robbery. Cards carrying the owner's fingerprints or personal identification numbers will do away even with credit-card theft. All banking will be done by phone and computer, and paper work by both consumer and bank will be a fraction of what it is today.

Because all purchases will be made by card and computer, checks will someday become extinct as well.

Because credit and debit cards will serve as the monetary system, all the frills and flourishes, the come-ons and enticements now being promoted by the credit-card systems will be gone, and interest rates will be lowered to a figure approaching sanity. No one will charge for a credit card.

American Express and Diners Club cards will primarily become business aids, and companies will use them for most offices purchases as well as for business travel and entertainment. These plans will not issue cards for personal use nor will either offer revolving credit. They will be a formidable part of the monetary exchange used for business. American Express will, most likely, emphasize domestic business needs while the Diners Club, if it is wise, will lay claim to being the true credit card for the international businessman and traveler.

The skeptics have always insisted that cash is needed, at least for everyday items such as newspapers and parking meters and mass transit.

In Houston, today, they are experimenting with pre-paid parking chits charged to your bank credit card and the New York mass transit system, as mentioned earlier, has introduced the same method for paying for subway transportation with the idea of expanding it to bus and train service. Fifty percent of the more than thirty thousand supermarkets in America now honor one or more all-purpose credit cards as do 80 percent of the country's department stores.

In California and other states, the credit-card purchase of gasoline has been made so simple that you never leave the pump to pay your bill. You merely insert your card into a machine attached to it, fill your tank, get your receipt, and drive away. You never see an attendant or a cashier.

Seven-Eleven now takes credit cards.

Shopping via television would be virtually nonexistent without credit cards. Television buying, usually a mistake, is quick-decision time. You see an item. You are talked into buying it. On impulse, you call in your order and your credit-card number.

If you had to write an order, make out a check, address an envelope, you would have time to reflect, more often than not, you'd forget the whole thing. Buying by television will grow, but credit-card companies will carefully scrutinize the offers and merchandise and the scams and junk products will be sifted out.

Some New York City taxis now accept credit cards.

Movie theaters honor credit cards as do sports events, legit theater, museums, concerts, and nearly every other kind of public event.

Burger King takes credit cards.

Industry estimates put credit-card volume at two trillion dollars by the year 2000. My own research suggests that the figure is conservative, partly because of the rapidly increasing acceptance by supermarkets and department stores and long-distance phone companies. But also because of the use of credit cards to pay federal income taxes. Corporate credit-card use for business and manufacturing needs will alone add substantially to any projections.

Of the more than one trillion dollars charged in 1993, $191.28 billion represented cash advances. Because the need for cash will decrease as credit-card acceptance expands, that figure will obviously decline.

"Hey!" someone asked us. "How about gambling, legal and otherwise?" Well, Jimmy Breslin's friend Fat

Thomas may well have been the first bookie to take an actual credit card as payment for a gambling loss, but be assured, he was not the last. In the midfifties, we discovered that a brothel in Puerto Rico was accepting Diners Club cards and reporting assignations as dinners and drinks. Certainly, bookies can and have been doing the same.

Legitimate gambling? Credit cardholders have always been able to get cash advances at money machines in Las Vegas or Atlantic City and a platinum or gold cardholder can dig deeply. In addition, casinos and racetracks all over the United States, including Indian reservations, have point-of-sale terminals which can immediately, with the swipe of a preferred credit card, emit a bank draft exchangeable for cash or chips.

"The American banking system has begun offering loans for the purpose of playing the horses," *Fortune* magazine moaned as far back as its October, 1980, issue.

At casinos, of course, cash needn't ever be seen since chips are the basic betting money. It would be simple, as well, for racetracks to issue betting chits to customers requesting advances.

Charge for postage stamps? It's already here.

Smart cards with computer chips in them will answer the problems of portability and privacy. You'll lend your brother-in-law money by inserting your card in his tiny home terminal—if you want to lend your brother-in-law money.

At the current time, 80 percent of the 360 billion retail and service transactions in the United States each year are paid for with cash. Ninety percent of those cash purchases involve amounts of less than twenty dollars.

The microchip charge card with a stored credit which can be replenished handily will accommodate those purchases with ease if the credit card we use doesn't.

But the credit card, even without a microchip or stored credit, is almost there now.

The card can be used for everything from burgers to income taxes. It can do something else that must be addressed. It can get even more people who tend to spend themselves into trouble.

If people can take their time in paying their taxes, they will, and they'll continue to buy things they might otherwise have avoided. The government reluctantly does give leeway on paying taxes now and charges 7 percent interest if you're late—a figure substantially lower than paid to card issuers for revolving credit—but people have a tendency to pay the government more promptly than their credit-card bills.

So this widespread acceptance, which has come and will continue to grow even more rapidly, is changing our monetary system and our lives. It's making things more simple and good living more available to us, and it's making a helluva lot of money for the credit-card companies. The potential for the profits for credit card issuers is mind boggling. Where will it go? Well, in 1993 it is estimated that all issuing U.S. companies realized combined profits on credit-card operations greater than the combined '93 profits of the American automotive industry giants, Ford, Chrysler, and GM.

The Justice Department has suddenly noticed that Visa and MasterCard, for the most part owned by the same banks, are, in a sense, competing with themselves and despite the public battles between the card compa-

nies and the wrangling over interest rates by the bank
issuers, might be guilty of price fixing. Late in 1994, the
American Bankers Association received a civil inves-
tigative demand from the Justice Department, the equivalent of a subpoena. Visa and MasterCard had already
been notified that the government was looking into possible antitrust violations.

"It's nothing," said the credit-card executives we
spoke to. And one tends to agree that while it may be
something, it will lead to nothing. Antitrust protection
has hardly been in vogue in recent decades. Caveat
emptor, and let him fend for himself.

Some are concerned with where so much reliance on
credit cards is taking us. Are the banks becoming "the
company store"? Are we sliding more and more into
debt?

When cash was the money of choice, we made our
own decisions, and most of us spent what we had in
hand or, at least, in the bank.

Now we can spend more than we have.

Well, maybe, say the banks, but it's not as serious a
problem as one would think and solutions are at hand.

Many in the credit-card industry feel that fears of
credit cards creating a nation of overspenders might
make colorful reading but they're blown out of pro-
portion. "Sure, the cards offer an obvious capability to
overspend," says MasterCard's Ed Hogan, "but the
lion's share of cardholders use them with care and
responsibility. Most credit-card problems come not
from abusers but from people whose world suddenly
caved in on them—loss of job, death in the family, ill-

ness. Those are people in circumstances that would cause financial problems even if there were no credit cards."

Hogan, like most in the industry, is excited about the microchip-based payment smart card.

He and others I spoke with wax enthusiastically over the card of the future which, among other things, will store and evaluate a person's financial ability to pay for what they're charging. "Chip-card technology," says Hogan, "will prevent abuse of the card by installing controls right in the bearer's own credit card. There will be no lag time on reporting purchases. The card and the networks will be able to know and evaluate each use immediately."

The cards will be getting smarter and smarter. Will we keep pace with them, or will they be telling us how much to spend, what to spend it on, where to spend it?

It's a soothsayer's lot to examine the inevitable, even if it portends gloom.

Is "Big-Brother" a credit card?

If he is, no one seems to be too concerned about it. Where once there was caution about predicting growth, now there is none. Card growth in this country has no boundaries, and growth around the rest of the world, according to MasterCard's Gene Lockhart, will even be greater.

"Particularly in Latin America and Asia-Pacific," he says. "I recently asked one of the five most powerful bankers in China how many credit cards would be in the hands of his countrymen by the year 2,000. He thought for a moment, then said, 'one hundred million.'"

Diners Club President Bob Rosseau predicts almost the same number for India. "Ten percent of the population in that country has a standard of living equal to or greater than the average person in the U.S. And that population is 850 million—that's 85 million people who can afford to use credit cards."

I feel like the mother of a nine year old who says, "I love you, but wash your hands—and keep your shoes off the bed—and, by the way, do your homework!"

Credit cards are one of the best ideas ever dreamed up. Cash and checks have seen their day. Their inadequacies have been covered here thoroughly. Anybody who's ever lost a wallet with cash in it or bounced a check because of poor arithmetic or tried to get one cashed in a place where nobody knows you can attest to that.

The banks are choking with checks. The credit card has and will alleviate, and eventually eradicate, that problem.

The effect a cashless society will have on robbery and drug traffic and violence and murder is incalculable. No cash—not much to rob. It's a solution Washington might want to ponder. It's better than building more jails.

But the credit-card companies still have to wash *their* hands, keep their shoes off the bed, and, most importantly, do their homework.

Credit cards offering revolving credit must be given out with more care. Pre-approved card solicitation should be discontinued.

The practice of giving blank checks to marginal credit risks must also be halted. Cardholders, given the right to charge, must clearly have the ability to pay for those charges at the time they are made. Credit-card charges should not be considered loans. They are conveniences, not dreams.

Those who do not clearly have the wherewithal to pay for charges at the time they're made should have debit cards, but debit cards should be given on a more equitable basis with the bank issuer paying decent interest on the money they're holding (and using) and charging less interest when revolving credit is used.

The secured card is a farce and should be discontinued if for no other reasons than they are unfair to the cardholder—even if he has bad credit—and make the bank look like the Mafia on the docks of Hoboken.

The smart card and other electronic innovations will make the debit card even a surer bet for the banks because a cardholder will at no time be able to charge more than they've deposited.

If the marginal credit risk is switched to debit cards and new hi-tech systems virtually do away with charging over limits and with fraud, all credit-card issuers should sharply reduce interest rates.

The card issuers should police those merchants and services using the cards as a tool to entice instant buying. Such endorsement should be given with care. No more bedsprings that build muscles or other phony mail-order and TV scams.

One bank card—at the most two—should be adequate for any cardholder. It should be impossible for an applicant to get more. No one needs eight or ten or a dozen credit cards. A central-monitoring service certainly should be able to control such overindulgence. The credit bureau need reworking. They're obviously incompetent and cavalier.

Such a limit will do away with the now-popular game of paying for one card's bills with another.

The credit-card companies themselves should stop acting like pitchmen, stop the intermural bickering, and start behaving like the institutions that control the monetary system and thus, control the world, because they will.

Growth will happen. The card issuers should concentrate on responsibility and restraint—theirs as well as the cardholders. They have a duty to their cardholders not to give them an open invitation to destroy themselves. Credit-card issuers should not equate themselves with merchants whose primary job is to get people to buy their wares and services; they should promote care and moderation. If beer companies do it, why not banks? Issuers cannot absolve themselves of that duty. They can't assume the attitude that credit losses will be taken care of nicely by volume, as has happened. Their obligation must be to the cardholder as well as to their bottom line.

The government should get into the act.

There should be a federal limit on interest rates on credit cards well below the approximately 16 percent now being charged by the average card issuer and certainly substantially below the 19.8 percent being charged by such giants as Bank of America, Great Western, and others. Interest on debit cards should be

regulated so that it is are more equitable to the cardholder.

On the other hand, penalties for late payments or for
the exceeding of credit limits are not only justifiable but
serve as an important and costly reminder to the cardholder who is overextending himself. The bank should
be allowed to charge whatever penalties are necessary
to protect themselves.

The holder of credit cards cannot and should not
depend on either the card issuers or the government to
protect them once they get the cards. The cards, inviting the holder to lead the good life, don't stint, travel,
wine, dine, buy that and enjoy this, hold their own
obvious dangers. The card is the siren, ever enticing
and clearly addictive.

As the population grows more and more dependent
on credit cards, there will be more enticements and
more reasons to, literally, go for broke. One would hope
that people will grow wiser and clearly understand the
problems and responsibilities as well as the convenience and simplicity and usefulness that they bring.

More importantly, the card issuers have to wise up.
Only greed and stupidity can stop the coming of the
total credit-card age. In their rush for profits and
growth, the card issuers must first realize that care and
judgment will, in the long run, give them even-greater
growth and larger profits and not create a debtor society
that, inevitably, will take the new currency, or at least
its management, out of their hands. Continued indis-
criminate distribution of cards, particularly of many
cards to a single holder, can truly lead to a credit-card
catastrophe. To many, it's already a catastrophe.

The great thing about cash is you can't spend more of it than you have. Credit cards must, within reason, offer the same sense of responsibility.

Nothing in the twenty-first century seems more inevitable or makes more sense than a society in which credit cards replace cash. There is no reason, except for man's own frailties, why this should not happen.

If February 8, 1950, the day that Frank MacNamara first tried out his credit-card idea, wasn't the day that cash died, it certainly started it on its descent into its grave.

NEW ITEM: As of June 30, 1994, credit-card charges in the United States alone increased by nearly 23 percent over 1993. It is estimated that charges around the rest of the world have increased at an even-greater pace.

INDEX

AAA, 164
Abt, Michelle, 215
Adelman, Phil, 245
Adler, Buddy, 85
affinity cards, 155
American Airlines, 156
    AAdvantage Plan, 155,
        164–65
American Association of
    Retired People, 210
American Banker, 122, 265
American Bankers
    Association, 137, 276
American Credit Collector's
    Association, 142
American Express, 37, 39,
    74–75, 93, 95, 104, 106–07,
    126–28, 149, 187–98, 206,
    232, 233, 272
    buying out Diners club,
        looks into, 62
    history of, 57–59
    issues own credit card,
        67–69
    second–class postage rate,
        fight for, 70–71
American Institute of Certified
    Public Accountants, 171–72
antitrust action against Visa
    and MasterCharge, possible,
    125–26, 275–76
Arkansas Federal, 165, 166, 211
*Around the World in Eighty
    Days,* 49

Asch, Jules, 104
Ascher, Sid, 19
AT&T, 155, 156, 168
    Universal card, 209
Atherton, William, 240–42
Ausobol, Lawrence M., 174
Automobile Club of California,
    210
Avco, 125
Ayob, Kenneth , 241–42
Ballard, Jerry, 141, 142
BankAmericard, 93, 116–17,
    123
Bank Cardholders of America,
    173, 225
Bank cards, 115–26, 149–54,
    188
    interest rate disparities,
        165–67, 172–75
Bank of America, 116–17, 123,
    170, 184, 185
Bank of China, 170
Bank One, 166
Barclay Bank, 170
Bellamy, Edward, 11, 25–26,
    86
Bennett, John, 124–25
Big Progam, The, 46
Billingsley, Sherman, 36–37
Black, Joanne, 220
Bloomingdale, Alfred, 31, 34,
    42, 46, 49, 51–53, 62–63, 65,
    66, 67, 71–72, 81–82, 85,
    101–02, 103, 104, 107–09

Allah Be Praised, produces, 52
buys out MacNamara, 34
Bloomingdale, Betsy , 63, 108
Borghese, Franco, 36
Bradford, Pete, 65
Brandenberger, Phil, 146–47
Breslin, Jimmy, 43–46
Brooks, Ernie, 19–20
Brown, Kathleen, 221
Budget and Credit Counseling
Services, 227
Budget Rent–a–Car, 30
Byrne, John J., 191
CardTrak, 185
Carte Blanche, 39, 54, 74,
76–80, 125, 201
Catling, Luther R., 227
Cavanagh, Walter, 207–08
Cawley, Charles, 171–72
Chase Manhattan Bank, 104,
157, 170, 184
Chase Reward Consolidator,
167, 210
Chemical Bank, 137, 156, 184
Shell MasterCard, 210
China, 153
Choice Bank, 166
Citibank, 123, 139, 164–65,
168–70, 184, 185–86, 187,
196, 200
Citicorp, 125–26, 135, 169–70
Clark, Howard, 61–62, 63, 65,
75, 81–82, 93, 126
Clark, Jack, 231
co–branding, 155–57, 162, 167
computer billing
American Express
introduces, 95
Diners Club converts to,
102–03

Consumer Credit Counseling
Service, 234
Continental Bank, 118, 119,
120
Continental Insurance
Company, 103, 105–06,
107, 125–26
Cooperthwaite and Sons, 11
Copacabana nightclub, 51
Credit Card Collector, 141
"credit–carditis," 134
Credit Card Management, 192,
220, 263
Credit Card News, The, 168
credit cards
affinity cards, 155
average number held by
Americans, 211
bad debts, 206–07
bankruptcy and, 223–24,
231, 234–35
debt, 223–36
fingerprint images, 137
fraud, 118–119, 135, 137,
142–43, 239–43
holograms, 143
secured, 184–86
sweepstakes and, 247–50
Daley, James, 168
Davis, Sammy, Jr., 50–51
debit card, 125, 181–84
MetroCard, 139
welfare recipients, for, 138
Debtor's Anonymous, 235
Dine and Sign, 31, 34
Diners Club, 21–23, 26–31,
33– 37, 39–41, 46–47,
53–55, 61, 68–69, 81–82,
93–94, 95, 106–07, 125–26,
153, 188, 193, 196, 197,
198–200, 206, 252, 272

cardboard credit cards,
early, 49
computer billing, converts
to, 102–03
foreign franchises, 37, 200
idea was conceived, story
of how, 26
Milwaukee restaurant
revolt, 40
reimbursement plan to
restaurants, 22
start–up investment, 17
Diners Club–Fugazy travel
agencies, 103, 107
Diners Club Magazine, 30, 35,
41, 42, 49, 70–71, 75, 107
"Diners Club News," 30
Dio, Frankie, 252
Discover card, 134, 149,
176–78, 196
Downey's restaurant, 43, 45
Doyle, Kenneth O., 216
Dumas, James, 223–24
Eastern Airlines, 48–49
El Borracho restaurant, 19, 20
Electronic Card, 125
Eley, Glen E., 217
Empire State Building, 27
E Pay, 146
European–American Bank.
See Franklin National Bank
Falwell, Jerry, 144
Fargo, William, 58, 59
Federal Reserve, 122, 162
bank card study, 1968, 120–21
Federal Trade Commission,
137, 138
First USA, 174
Fisher, Art, 96
Five Percent Club, 215

Flatbush National Bank, 181
Fleet Bank of Hartford, 211
Florida Marlins, The, 142
Ford Motor Company, 163,
168
Franklin National Bank, 115
Freudberg, Raymond, 245–46
Friedman, Mokey, 42
Fry, Dave, 104
FTC. See Federal Trade
Commission.
General Electric, 163–64
General Motors, 155–56,
162–63, 168, 210
General Petroleum, 12
Goldmeyer, David, 245
Golub, Harvey, 191
Goodman, Jordan, 264–65
Goulden, Joseph C., 232–33
Great Western Bank, 166
Greenberg, Hank, 50–51
Griffin, Alice, the dachsund,
118
Gurney, Kathleen, 217
Hamilton Credit Corporation,
22–23
Hammer, Robert K., 175, 265
Hazard, Geoffrey, 217
Heard, J. Victor, 105–06
Henry Hudson Hotel, 30
Hilton, Barron, 71–73
Hilton Hotels, 71
Hinke, Karl, 121
Hock, Dee Ward, 123
Hogan, Ed, 262–63, 276
holograms
use on credit cards, 143
Home Savings Bank, 184
Household Bank, 176
Howard, Cy, 52

Hudson, Elizabeth, 230
Identicator Corporation, 137
Independent Card, The, 138
Interbank, 117, 121, 123
Interlink, Visa debit card, 182,
 183
Internal Revenue Service, 133
Japanese Credit Bureau (JCB),
 149, 175–76, 198
Jolley, Julie Marie, 241
Kaye, Danny, 86, 88, 90, 91
Kaye, Yvonne, 230–31
Keegan, Michael, 141
Kessler Exchange, 213
Kirkpatrick, Dick, 28, 55, 102
 billing system, devises, for
 Diners Club, 28
Kohn, Daniel, 147
Kraushaar, Judah, 173
Kutler, Jeff, 122–23, 183,
 265–66
Lackey, Lawrence, 46
Lane, Frank, 50
Larkin, Kenneth, 116
Levy, Gus, 65
Linklater, Richard, 214–15
Lively, Mike, 82
Lockhart, N. Eugene, 144,
 259–60, 277
Loen, Ernest, 103–04
Looking Backward: 2000 to
 1887, 11, 25–26
Lownes, Victor, 42
Lundquist, Weyman L., 140
MacNamara, Frank X., 13,
 16–17, 20–23, 25, 26–28,
 33–35, 37–38
Maestro debit card, 182, 183–4
Major's Cabin Grill
 Diners Club card used for
 first time, 16–17

Man from the Diners Club,
 The, 86, 88, 90–91
Marine Midland Bank, 171–72
Marquette Bank of
 Minneapolis, 123
MasterCard, 93, 122, 124–25,
 144, 150, 151–53, 154–56,
 188, 275–76
 lower credit standards, 154
 MasterCard II, 125
Mastercharge, 93, 117, 122,
 123, 124
Mazzei, Rudolph L., 251
MBNA, 170–72
McBride, Donald R., 121
McCrie, Robert, 260–61
McKinley, Robert, 172, 185, 216
Mellon Bank Corporation of
 Pittsburgh, 134
Merando, Joseph, 228–29
Mester, Loretta, 162
MetroCard, 139
Meyer, Martin, 213, 221
Midwest Bank Card, 118
Mierzwinski, Ed, 138
Miller, Mitchell, 219
Miraglia, Joseph, 76–80
Moger, Byron, 237
Mondex, 140
Morgan, Vicki, 108
Morley, Robert, 145
Muzychenko, Jay, 226
National Center for Financial
 Education, 213
National Foundation for
 Consumer Credit
 Counseling, 226, 234
Nationsbank of Atlanta, 165
New York City Transit
 Commission
 MetroCard, 139

Nilson, Spencer, 53, 55, 68, 149–50
Nilson Report, 143, 173, 175
Northeast Airlines, 47
Oak Brook Bank, 166
Operation Plastic Dragon, 243
Optima card, 151, 189–90, 209
True Grace card, 190, 191–92, 264–65
Patman, Wright, 119, 122
Penney, J.C., Company, 134
Playboy magazine, 42–43
Podell, Jules, 51
Pony Express, 58
Powell, Charley, 86
Proctor, Cynthia, 229
Proctor, Michael, 229
Proxmire, William, 119, 122
RAM Research Corporation, 172
Reed, Ralph, 59–62, 63–64, 65–66
Reilly, Jean, 233–34
Reise, Philip, 191, 192
Richard, Paul, 213–14
Richardson, Gary, 239
Richman, Bill, 36, 55, 69
Robinson, James, III, 126
Robinson, Philip J., 219
Rolling Stones' credit card, 135
Ross, Steve, 126, 220
Rosseau, Robert, 192, 261–62, 278
Roth, Arthur, 115
Russell, Chuck, 267
Santura, Robert, 250–51
Sanwa Bank, 185
Schaefer, Donald, 138
Schneider, Ralph, 16–17, 21–23, 29, 31, 33–36, 42–43,

47–48, 52–53, 62, 63–64, 65–66, 67–68, 71– 72, 76, 81–82, 96–97, 101–02, 157, 220
buys out MacNamara, 34
Schuler, Robert, 144
Schumer, Charles E., 218, 220
Scientology, Church of , 145
Sears, Roebuck and Company, 134, 176
secured credit card, 184–86
Sheraton Central Credit Card, 72, 73
Sheraton Hotels, 72–74
Shinbrot, Jeffrey S., 218–19
Signature magazine, 107
Signet Bank, 167
Simmons, Don, 18, 20, 23, 25–26, 35, 69, 87–88, 96
Simmons, Matty, 21–26, 29, 31, 35–37, 41–44, 45–46, 47–49, 51, 67–68, 69, 88, 96–97, 108, 128
early career, 18–20
American Express sale, opposed to, 64
leaves Diners Club, 104
Skillern, Frank, 191
"smart card," 140
Sonnenberg, Ben, 62
Southern New England Telephone, 155
Spiegel catologue company, 12, 209
Stewart, John, 219–20, 263–64
Stock, Craig, 227–28
Stork Club, 36
Sturdevant, James C., 140
Sturges, John, 119
Sulkes, M. Mark, 37
Sullivan, Ann, 224–25

Sullivan, Charlene, 225
Swaggart, Jimmy, 145
Swank, Elizabeth, 235
Tannauzzo, Michael, 250–51
Telemarketing
  credit card use in, 136
Tilem, Joe, 54–55, 75–76, 242
Titus, Joe, 39–40, 44, 50–51,
  55, 103, 219
Todd, Mike, 49
Tootelian, Dennis, 216
Toots Shor's, 13, 20, 37
Towbin, Belmont, 81, 102
Townsend, Bob, 61–62, 63, 64,
  74
Townsend, Robert, 214
Trip–Charge, 30, 34, 64, 65, 66
TRS (Travel Related Services,
  American Express), 195–96
TRW, 137
Tunks, Greg, 141
Twenty–first Century
  Communications, 108
U.S. Justice Department,
  275–76
U.S. Postal Service, 142

U.S. Public Interest Research
  Group, 138
Universal Air Travel Plan, 12
Universal Bank, 156
VeriFone, 143
Visa, 122, 124–25, 150,
  151–53, 154, 156, 161–62,
  177, 187, 188, 194, 275–76
Visa Interactive, 146
Wachovia Bank of Wilmington,
  166, 167
Ward, Peter, 225–26
Warren, Ted, 246
Waters, George, 75
  computer billing, intro-
  duces, 95
Watkins, James T., 234
Weiss, Seymour, 94
Wells, Henry, 57–58, 59
Wells Fargo and Company, 58
Wells Fargo Bank, 139–40, 185
Western Union, 12
Westminster Bank of England,
  104
Winsted, Connecticut, 87–90
Wood, Christopher, 267–68